I0159795

THE LAW
and the Believer

Biblical Proof that Believers are *not* Under the Law

Dirk Waren

Soaring Eagle Press

THE LAW and the Believer

Copyright © 2018 by Dirk Waren

All rights reserved. No original part of this book may be reproduced or transmitted in any form or by any means, electronic or mechanical, including photocopying, recording, or by any information storage and retrieval system, without the written permission of the Publisher, except where permitted by law.

Unless otherwise indicated, all Scripture quotations are taken from the Holy Bible, New International Version®. NIV®. Copyright © 1973, 1978, 1984, 2011 by the International Bible Society. Used by permission of Zondervan Bible Publishers.

Many NIV citations are from the 2011 Revised edition.

Other cited translations are listed in the Bibliography.

All underlining, italics and bracketed notes in scriptural citations are added by the author.

Pronominal references to Deity in this work are not always capitalized.

Edited by KEEII; and chapter 10 by J. Altieri.

ISBN: 978-0-578-43237-3
PUBLISHED BY SOARING EAGLE PRESS
Youngstown

Printed in the United States of America

...we have been released from the Law so that we serve in the new way of the Spirit, and not in the old way of the written code.

- Romans 7:6

CONTENTS

Introduction

The info in this book is crucial for every Christian's spiritual health. Too many believers today don't understand the difference between the inferior Old Covenant and the superior New Covenant. They don't realize God's purpose for the Law and what role it plays in the life of New Testament believers, as well as what role it doesn't play.

Because this material is so essential, key passages & points are reemphasized in later chapters. The purpose for doing this is so that believers "get it" and never forget it. It's to establish **a New Covenant foundation** that is so solid it's unbreakable and no false teacher who preaches a "different gospel" — one that mixes New Testament truths with the Mosaic Law — can damage it. The 1st century apostles practiced this as well because it effectively drives home key truths (see, for example, 2 Peter 1:12-13).

A secondary reason for a little reiteration is that — in a book like this — readers tend to jump to the chapter they're interested in and therefore miss vital data relayed in previous chapters. I don't assume that readers have read the prior chapters; as such, vital passages & points are sometimes repeated.

God Bless You as You Seek & Serve!

1

—

Believers are *NOT* Under The Law

There are quasi-Christian groups and denominations today whose goal is to put New Covenant believers *under* the Old Testament Law, which is also known as the Torah. A prime example is the Hebrew Roots movement.

The questions we want to tackle in this book are: What was the purpose of the Old Testament Law? Are believers "under" the Law, as the Israelites were in the Old Testament? If we're not *under* the Law, are we obligated to fulfill it? If so, what parts? And how exactly do we fulfill it if we're not under it? Also, how does the Law relate to the New Testament believer? And does it serve any purpose in the Church, the body of Christ on earth?

All these questions and more will be answered. Any doubts will be removed from your mind because the God-breathed Scriptures are clear and, as Christ put it, **the truth will make you free** (John 8:31-32).

Let's start with the fact that false teachers who try to put believers *under* the Law are nothing new. They've been around since the beginning of the Church. A good example from the Bible is…

The Judaizers who tried to corrupt the Galatian Churches

The "Judaizers" were Judaizing teachers, meaning a group of legalistic Jewish "Christians" who taught that the requirements of Jewish religion—the Mosaic Law plus other traditions—were necessary for salvation and spirituality. Their requirements included physical circumcision, traditional fasts and observing various holy-days. Circumcision was an issue as shown in Galatians 2:3 and 5:2-3, while the others are verified in Paul's criticism of the Galatian believers here:

You are observing special days and months and seasons and years!
Galatians 4:10

- **"days"** refers to strict Sabbath-keeping
- **"months"** to the fast initiated by the Jews during their Babylonian captivity
- **"seasons"** to the seven Jewish feast days
- **"years"** to the seven 7-year periods that climaxed with the fiftieth year, the year of Jubilee

Within this context, Paul emphasized the purpose of Christianity:

It is for freedom that Christ has set us free. Stand firm, then, and do not let yourselves be burdened again by a yoke of slavery.
Galatians 5:1

The "yoke of slavery" is a reference to the yoke of religious law—the Mosaic Law and the other Hebraic traditions noted.

Putting believers under such laws is a "different gospel," as Paul called it in Galatians 1:6. In other words, it's a perversion of the true gospel.

The true gospel is that salvation comes simply by God's graciousness through faith in Christ's justifying death and resurrection, "not by works so that no one can boast" (Ephesians 2:9). Genuine faith will produce good works (James 2:14-24) because "we are God's workmanship, created in Christ Jesus to do good works" (Ephesians 2:10). This occurs naturally as the believer learns to put off the old self — the flesh — and put on the new self (Ephesians 4:22-24).

Legalists Want to Put You into Bondage

The Judaizers who infiltrated the Galatian churches were legalists. They had a spirit of bondage, which made them obsessed with the yoke of religious law. A "yoke" is a device for joining together a pair of draft animals so they can be worked as a team, typically oxen. The beasts are shackled together for the purpose of work. That's what the yoke of religious law does to people; it shackles them to perform religious works. It's religious bondage, which is the antithesis of the Christian spirit of freedom and, as such, saps joy.

You won't see a lot of joy in those entrenched in religious slavery. The Judaizers were such people and they started to sap the Galatians' joy, which is why Paul asked them, "What happened to all your joy?" (Galatians 4:15).

Those who have a spirit of bondage *can't* set others free because they themselves aren't free. People can only give what they've got. Those who have a spirit of bondage can only give bondage. In fact, it's their primary objective — to make people slaves to religious laws. It's their goal. Here's an example:

> **...some <u>false brothers</u> had infiltrated our ranks to spy on <u>the freedom we have in Christ Jesus</u> and to <u>make us slaves</u>. [5] We did not give in to them for a moment,**
>
> **Galatians 2:4-5**

Here Paul is talking about his second trip to Jerusalem where he shared his calling with the leaders of the Jerusalem church. His calling was to minister to the Gentiles. That's when some legalists infiltrated Paul's group to spy on them. We know they were hardcore legalists because Paul describes them as "false brothers." In other words, these weren't genuine believers who were stumbling into a system of rules & regulations, like the Galatians, but rather full-tilt legalists, similar to the Pharisees who antagonized the Messiah during his earthly ministry. They weren't spiritual brothers at all.

And notice what their goal was: to make slaves of those who were walking in the freedom of Christ. Make no mistake, legalists hate freedom; it goes against everything they are. Legalists are people in bondage to rules, which is why it's called legal-ism, meaning law-ism or rule-ism.

Paul stresses in verse 5 that he and his team didn't give-in to these legalists for a moment. You cannot parley with people infected by this spiritual disease. If you give 'em an inch they'll take the proverbial mile. Resist their legalism, pray for them, correct them through the Scriptures, and leave them when you must, as Jesus taught in Matthew 15:14, but never give in to them, not a single inch.

The only exception would be if you're going into *their* territory to try to minister life to them. Paul expressed it this way: "Though I am free and belong to no man, I make myself a slave to everyone, to win as many as possible. To the Jews I became like a Jew, to win the Jews. To those under the law I became like one under the law (**though I myself am not under the law**), so as to win those under the law… To the weak I became weak, to win the weak. I have become all things to all men so that by all possible means I might save some. I do all this for the sake of the gospel, that I may share in its blessings" (1 Corinthians 9:19-20,22-23).

Christians are NOT *Under* the Old Testament Law (Torah)

As noted earlier, the Judaizers who infiltrated the Galatian assemblies wanted to put the believers back *under* the Old Testament Law, along with other Jewish religious traditions. The name 'Judaizers' comes from Galatians 2:14 where Paul publicly corrected Peter for forcing Gentile believers "to follow Jewish customs." The phrase "to follow Jewish customs" is one word in the Koine Greek *ioudaizó (ee-oo-dah-ID-zoh)*, which means "to Judaize," that is, "to live like a Jew." So a 'Judaizer' is someone who tries to get people to live like a Jew under the Law.

A good modern example of Judaizers is the legalists of the Hebrew Roots movement, who have infiltrated many assemblies and seminaries. Yet notice how clear the New Testament is about believers not being under the Mosaic Law, the Torah:

> But if you are led by the Spirit, <u>you are not under the law.</u>
>
> **Galatians 5:18**

> For sin shall not be your master, because <u>you are not under law</u>, but under grace.
>
> **Romans 6:14**

> **...we have been <u>released from the law</u> so that we serve in the new way of the Spirit, and <u>not</u> <u>in the old way of the written code</u>.**
>
> **Romans 7:6**

In the New Testament era we've been released from the Law — the Torah — to "serve in the new way of the Spirit, and not in the old way of the written code." **We are "not under Law, but under grace,"** meaning we're under God's graciousness — God's favor — through the work of Christ wherein we obtain spiritual regeneration and are reconciled with the LORD, not to mention indwelt by the Counselor, the Holy Spirit.

What does being "under the law" mean? It means putting the Law in front of you and trying to force yourself to comply. The problem with this is that it doesn't work. In fact, it will actually increase the sin problem; and the bulk of the Old Testament testifies to this. Why do you think Paul said, "The law was added **so that the trespass might increase**" (Romans 5:20)? You see, "the power of sin is the law" (1 Corinthians 15:56). The Law not only arouses sinful passions (Romans 7:5), but exposes our inability to live up to God's standard and hence prepares us to admit our need for grace. This was the reason the Law was given to humanity — to increase the sin problem and drive us to the Savior in whom we can have spiritual regeneration. Yes, the Law "is holy, righteous and good" — no doubt — but God uses it to illustrate humanity's wretched sinful condition and drive us to Christ (Romans 7:12).

Since believers are justified in God's sight by faith we are no longer under the supervision of the Law:

> **So the law was our guardian <u>until</u> <u>Christ came</u> that we might be justified by faith. [25] Now that this faith has come, <u>we are no longer under a guardian</u>.**   **Galatians 3:24-25**

'Guardian' is translated as "tutor" in some translations and as "schoolmaster" in the King James Version. The original Greek word refers to a household servant or slave whose job was to tutor and oversee male children until they came of age whereupon they took on the responsibilities and freedoms of adulthood. Are you getting this? Believers are no longer under the supervision of the Mosaic Law (and religious law in general). Since we are spiritually regenerated and have the Holy Spirit we are liberated to function in the responsibilities and freedoms of spiritual adulthood.

New Covenant Believers are Under the Law of Christ

While New Testament believers are not under the Mosaic Law, **we are under the law of Christ**:

> **Though I am free and belong to no one, I have made myself a slave to everyone, to win as many as possible. [20] To the Jews I became like a Jew, to win the Jews. To those under the law I became like one under the law (though <u>I myself am not under the law</u>), so as to win those under the law. [21] To those not having the law I became like one not having the law (though I am not free from God's law but <u>am under Christ's law</u>), so as to win those not having the law.**
>
> **1 Corinthians 9:19-21**

As you can see, the apostle Paul was "under Christ's law," not under the Mosaic Law. He only became "like one under the law" on certain occasions in order to "win those under the law," meaning he did so to win Jews over to the superior New Covenant. We'll look at what makes the New Covenant 'superior' momentarily.

So believers are not under the Old Testament Law, but rather "under Christ's law." Here's another passage that verifies this:

> **Carry each other's burdens, and in this way you will fulfill <u>the law of Christ</u>.**
>
> **Galatians 6:2**

But what is the law of Christ? Neither of these verses defines it. Thankfully, this isn't a problem because **Scripture interprets Scripture** and the rest of the New Testament shows us what the law of Christ is. Notice Jesus' answer to an Expert in the Law who sought to test him:

> **"Teacher, which is the greatest commandment in the Law?"**
> **[37]Jesus replied: " 'Love the Lord your God with all your heart and with all your soul and with all your mind.' [38] This is the first and greatest commandment. [39] And the second is like it: 'Love your neighbor as yourself.' [40] <u>All the Law and the Prophets hang on these two commandments</u>."**
>
> **Matthew 22:36-40**

"The law and the prophets" is a reference to the Old Testament Scriptures; and, specifically, to the moral Law since the dietary and ceremonial laws of the Old Testament were **foreshadows of Christ** and were fulfilled in Him...

The Law Foreshadowed the Reality, Christ

Observe what this key passage clearly states:

> **Therefore do not let anyone judge you by
> what you eat or drink, or with regard to a
> religious festival, a New Moon celebration or a
> Sabbath day.** [17] <u>**These are a shadow of the things
> that were to come**</u>**; the** <u>**reality**</u>**, however, is found
> in Christ.**
>
>   **Colossians 2:16-17**

The passage is addressing the dietary and ceremonial laws of the Old Testament: "what you eat or drink" refers to dietary laws and the others refer to ceremonial laws. We are not to allow legalists to judge us negatively by these things. In fact, all of them — dietary laws, the Jewish festivals, the New Moon celebration and the Sabbath day — were **mere shadows of what was to come**, meaning **Jesus Christ**, the Anointed One.

"A shadow" means a foreshadow, which is something that testifies to the reality to come. The real thing, however, is not the shadow. "The reality is found in Christ" and if you're a believer YOU are "in Christ." Are you following?

Everything in the Law and Prophets from Genesis to Malachi were types & shadows of the true reality, which is Christ, and the spiritual rebirth that comes through his seed, not to mention the corresponding indwelling/empowerment of the Holy Spirit. More than 600 laws were given to the Hebrews in the Old Testament and Jesus fulfilled every one of them; he completed or stopped each one of them, including the Sabbath. This is why Scripture blatantly says "Christ is the culmination [end] of the law so that there may be righteousness for everyone who believes" (Romans 9:4).

So the dietary and ceremonial laws were fulfilled in Christ and thus we are "released from" them (Romans 7:6). Of course, we are released from the moral law as well since the Messiah also fulfilled the moral law. As such, we're not *under* the moral Law. But...

Not being Under the Law is NOT a License to Sin

Now, some dubious types might think that this gives them a license to sin, but Paul dealt with this same question in the 1st century and notice his response:

> **What then? Shall we sin because we are not under the law but under grace? By no means!**
>
> **Romans 6:15**

So, while believers are not under the moral law, we uphold it:

> **Do we, then, nullify the law by this faith? Not at all! Rather, <u>we uphold the law</u>.**
>
> **Romans 3:31**

Believers Fulfill the Law by Walking in the Spirit

How exactly do we uphold the moral law; that is, establish it and fulfill it? Observe…

> **so that <u>the righteous standard of the Law</u> might be fulfilled in us, <u>who do not live according to the flesh but according to the spirit</u>.**
>
> **Romans 8:4** (BSB)

The "righteous standard of the Law" refers to the moral Law, which is fulfilled in believers "who do not live according to the flesh, but according to the spirit." This means learning to live out of your new spiritual nature as led of the Holy Spirit:

> **So I say, walk by the spirit, and you will**
> **not gratify the desires of the flesh.**
> > **Galatians 5:16**

You see? Walking in the spirit is the key to fulfilling the moral law for the New Testament believer. Walking in the spirit is one-in-the-same as "participating in the divine nature" (2 Peter 1:4). It means being spirit-controlled rather than flesh-ruled and is the automatic result of loving God, which is the primary part of the law of Christ and includes "coming near to God" (James 4:8). If you are "near to God" that obviously means that you have a close relationship. So **relationship with the LORD is paramount**.

New Covenant Believers are NOT "Lawless"

I need to interject something here: modern-day Judaizers who advocate being *under* the Old Testament Law argue that Christians who focus on God's grace in Christ rather than Torah are "lawless" because sin *is* lawlessness (1 John 3:4). However, we clearly see above that genuine Christians are not lawless but, in fact, **we fulfill the righteous standard of the moral Law by living according to the spirit and not the flesh**. Learning to master walking-in-the-spirit is a process in our spiritual journey. We improve at it as we grow.

Of course we all miss it, which is what 'sin' literally means — missing the mark in the sense of a moral failure. But because Christ died for all of our sins, God forgives us when we humbly confess and purifies us of "all unrighteousness" (1 John 1:8-9). (This passage points out, by the way, that anyone who says they *never* miss it is a liar). If God forgives believers and cleanses them of *all* unrighteousness when they 'fess up, what's that make them? Completely righteous in God's sight which means they're not "lawless," as Judaizers argue. No, they're *righteous* in Christ.

Christianity is Two Rules with Three Applications

Let's get back to the Messiah's statement in Matthew 22:

> **Jesus replied: " 'Love the Lord your God with all your heart and with all your soul and with all your mind.' [38] This is the first and greatest commandment. [39] And the second is like it: 'Love your neighbor as yourself.' [40] <u>All the Law and the Prophets hang on these two commandments</u>."**
>
> **Matthew 22:37-40**

All the Old Testament moral laws can be condensed into two basic rules with three applications: LOVE GOD and LOVE PEOPLE as you LOVE YOURSELF. When you do this you automatically fulfill *all* the moral law of the Old Testament, which is verified by several passages:

> **"In everything, then, do to others as you would have them do to you. For <u>this is the essence of the Law and the prophets</u>."   Matthew 7:12**

> **Let no debt remain outstanding, except the continuing debt to love one another, for <u>whoever loves others has fulfilled the law</u>. [9] The commandments, "You shall not commit adultery," "You shall not murder," "You shall not steal," "You shall not covet," and whatever other command there may be, <u>are summed up in this one command</u>: "Love your neighbor as yourself." [10] <u>Love does no harm to a neighbor. Therefore love is the fulfillment of the law.</u>**
>
> **Romans 13:8-10**

The entire Law is fulfilled in a single decree: "Love your neighbor as yourself."

Galatians 5:14

The law of Christ or law of love is also referred to as "the royal law" in Scripture:

If you really keep the royal law found in Scripture, "Love your neighbor as yourself," you are doing right.

James 2:8

John explained the law of love like so: "God is love. Whoever lives in love lives in God, and God in them" (1 John 4:16).

I should add that loving others means walking in **tough love** when necessary just as much as it means walking in **gentle love**. There are several clear examples in Scripture of both Jesus and the apostles walking in tough love when appropriate (e.g. Matthew 23:13-35, Mark 11:15-18, Acts 8:17-24, 13:8-12 and Galatians 2:11-14).

These Two Commandments are *One* Command — the Law of Love

Notice how John referred to these first two commandments as **one command**:

Dear friends, if our hearts do not condemn us, we have confidence before God [22] and receive from him anything we ask, because we keep his commands and do what pleases him. [23] And this is his command: to believe in the name of his

Son, Jesus Christ, and to love one another as he commanded us.
1 John 3:21-23

Two things need stressed:

1. John defines keeping the Lord's commands as fulfilling the twofold command of love—loving God and loving people.
2. To "keep his command*s*" in verse 22 is referred to as **one command** in verse 23. What command is this? The **command of love**, which is **the law of Christ**. This can be observed in another of John's letters:

And this is <u>love</u>: that we walk in obedience to <u>his commands</u>. As you have heard from the beginning, <u>his command</u> is that you <u>walk in love</u>.
2 John 1:6

Whenever the New Testament speaks of fulfilling the Lord's commands it's talking about this law of love. See John 15:10,12 and 1 John 4:21 for two good examples. These passages are never talking about keeping the Ten Commandments or the other moral commands of the 613 Torah laws. Why? Because when we fulfill the law of Christ — the law of love — we automatically fulfill *all* the moral commandments of the Old Testament. You see? Biblical Christianity is simple as pie.

It's interesting that in verse 23 John defines the first and greatest command — to love God (Matthew 22:37-38) — as "**believe** in the name of his Son, Jesus Christ." Jesus did the same thing at the Last Supper:

> "A **new command** I give you: **Love one another**. As I have loved you, so you must love one another. [35] By this everyone will know that you are my disciples, if you love one another."
>
> **John 13:34-35**

Shortly later he adds:

> "**Believe Me** that I am in the Father and the Father is in Me—or at least **believe** on account of the works themselves."
>
> **John 14:11**

He then concludes:

> "If you love me, keep **my commands**."
>
> **John 14:15**

What commands? The two commands he just gave: **1.** Love one another and **2.** believe in him. You see, "keeping the Lord's commands" in the New Testament *always* refers to the law of love, which is the law of Christ. It never refers to being under the Mosaic Law.

But why do both John and Jesus refer to loving God in terms of *believing*? Because believing in God is not like believing in leprechauns or fairy tales. Everything in creation screams out that God exists (Psalm 19:1-4 & Romans 1:18-20). To suggest that everything in the universe came about through accident and that there's no Intelligent Designer is a slap in the face to the Almighty. It's like expecting a Boeing 747 to emerge out of a metal scrapyard after millions of years, which is absurd.

Unfortunately, as Paul put it, unbelievers "are darkened in their understanding and separated from the life of God because of the ignorance that is in them due to the hardening of their hearts"

(Ephesians 4:18). In other words, they have faith but they've willingly hardened their hearts to it, consciously or subconsciously. Why? For a number of reasons, such as not wanting to give up some pet sin, but often simply because that's how their godless culture has brainwashed them, and they choose to run with the pack because it's the easiest path. So they deny obvious reality.

But why is faith linked to loving God and receiving salvation? Because faith is nothing more or less than believing God. That's precisely what Adam & Eve failed to do when they were tested in the Garden of Eden and that's why they fell (see Genesis 2:15-3:24). In other words, **the fall of humanity came about due to unbelief and therefore humanity's restoration is dependent upon belief**.

Why is **belief in Jesus Christ and his work** so crucial, as noted above by John and Jesus? Because it's through Christ and his work that the Almighty is able to reconcile with humanity, graciously offering us **1.** forgiveness of sins, **2.** reconciliation and **3.** eternal life. Anyone who loves God will recognize and accept this awesome gift while anyone who doesn't will stubbornly reject it.

The New Covenant is SUPERIOR to the Old Covenant

God works with humanity through covenants, which means 'agreement' or 'contract.' [1] Such agreements always have terms. As noted earlier, the New Covenant that believers have with God is superior to the Old Covenant that the Israelites had:

---

[1] We observe in the Bible the Adamic Covenant, the Noahic Covenant, the Abrahamic Covenant, the Mosaic Covenant and the New Covenant.

> They serve at a sanctuary that is a copy and shadow of what is in heaven. This is why Moses was warned when he was about to build the tabernacle: "See to it that you make everything according to the pattern shown you on the mountain." [6] But in fact <u>the ministry Jesus has received is as superior to theirs as the covenant of which he is mediator is superior to the old one,</u> since the new covenant is established on better promises...
>
> [13] <u>By calling this covenant "new," he has made the first one obsolete</u>; and what is obsolete and outdated will soon disappear.
>
> **Hebrews 8:5-6,13**

The New Covenant is "superior" because we've been released from the Law — the Torah — as shown in Romans 7:6. We serve in the new way of the Spirit wherein we receive spiritual regeneration (Ephesians 4:22-24) and not in the Old Covenant way of the written code, i.e. the Law. This is great because "the letter kills, but the Spirit gives life" (2 Corinthians 3:6).

Humble repentance & faith are the conditions for entering into the New Covenant (Acts 20:21 & Hebrews 6:1) and the terms are "faith working through love," which means faith is activated or energized by love (Galatians 5:6 Amplified). When we walk out of love (1 Corinthians 13:4-7) we walk out of faith and thus negate it, which isn't good because faith is the foundation of our covenant. Why is "faith working through love" so important? Because love is the fulfillment of the moral Law. It's the law of Christ, the law of love.

Needless to say, if you come across a church, a group or an individual that advocates believers being *under* the Old Testament Law — including observing the Saturday Sabbath — flee for your spiritual welfare. These types adhere to a "different gospel"

(Galatians 1:6). Some obvious modern examples include: The Hebrew Roots movement, adherents of Armstrongism (e.g. the United Church of God and the Philadelphia Church of God) and the Seventh-Day Adventists.

"The Letter Kills, but the Spirit Gives Life"

We saw above that "the letter kills, but the Spirit gives life," which contrasts the inferiority of the Old Covenant with the Superiority of the New Covenant (2 Corinthians 3:6). This passage goes on to describe the Old Covenant as "the ministry of death" and "the ministry of condemnation" (verses 7 & 9 ESV). Why? Because there was no possibility of redemption through the Mosaic Law. It's very purpose was to reveal humanity's desperate sinful condition and "the wages of sin is death." The best answer the Law could give for serious sins like adultery, homosexuality, juvenile rebellion, blasphemy and witchcraft was to **KILL the offender**. Observe for yourself in these blunt passages: Leviticus 20:10, Deuteronomy 22:22, Leviticus 20:13, Deuteronomy 21:18-21, Leviticus 24:13-14, Exodus 22:18 and Leviticus 20:27.

These severe laws were specifically for those under the Old Covenant in the Israelite community. The purpose of these laws was to protect Hebrew society by eliminating the offender and thus eliminating the spread of the sin in question since people tend to imitate the example set by others (in other words, sin spreads socially). Unlike the superior New Covenant, there was no provision for a new nature in Christ along with the empowering of the Holy Spirit and so the strict answer of the Torah was to execute the perpetrator, which was good in that it provided swift justice and protected society.

I'm sure you see the problem with going back to the Old Covenant. For instance, if we instituted today the law to stone to death stubbornly rebellious youths there'd be a lot less teenagers around (and I personally would've never survived my teen years)! Praise God for the spiritual rebirth and redemption that's available through Christ — truly, "the Spirit gives **life**"! I'm living testimony. ☺

You are NOT Under the Law!

The purpose of this chapter was to clearly establish from God's Word that **New Testament believers are *not* under the Old Testament Law**, rather we fulfill the moral law through the law of Christ, which is the law of love — LOVING GOD and LOVING PEOPLE as we LOVE OURSELVES.

I encourage you to go over this material until you master the key points, particularly the passages that explicitly state that New Covenant believers are not under the Law. If you do this, no modern-day Judaizer will be able to derail your walk with their unbiblical legalistic drivel. Amen.

2

"Law is Made <u>Not</u> for the Righteous"

Many believers may find this surprising, but the Old Testament Law — the Torah — was not made for the righteous. Note what the New Testament reveals in this regard:

> **We know that the law is good <u>if one uses it properly.</u> [9] We also know that <u>law is made not for the righteous</u> but for lawbreakers and rebels, the ungodly and sinful, the unholy and irreligious; for those who kill their fathers or mothers, for murderers, [10] for adulterers and perverts, for slave traders and liars and perjurers—and for whatever else is contrary to the sound doctrine [11] that conforms to the glorious gospel of the blessed God,**
>
> **1 Timothy 1:8-11**

This passage starts off by declaring that the Law is good, but only if it is used properly. This means that the Law is

intrinsically "holy, righteous and good," as Paul pointed out in
Romans 7:12, but it is only good for people if it is used properly.
In other words, in and of itself the law is good, but **it is only good
for people when it is appropriately applied**. The remaining
verses reveal what this means…

The Old Testament Law is *not* made for the righteous. Who
are "the righteous"? This refers to New Covenant believers
because we are made righteous in Christ through spiritual rebirth:

> **God made him who had no sin to be sin for us, so
> that in him we might become the righteousness
> of God.**
>
> **2 Corinthians 5:21**

Jesus never sinned, but he became sin for us on the cross so
that in him we might become the righteousness of God. 'Become'
in the Greek is a form of *ginomai (JIN-oh-may)*, which means "to
come into being, to be born." Whether you know it or not, when
you turned to the LORD in repentance and faith you were
spiritually reborn and, consequently, **your spirit was born the
righteousness of God**. This explains why we are instructed to put
off the flesh and put on the new man — meaning live out of our
reborn spirit — because it was "created to be *like* God in true
righteousness and holiness." Let's look at this potent passage:

> **You were taught, with regard to your former
> way of life, to put off your old self, which is being
> corrupted by its deceitful desires; [23] to be made
> new in the attitude of your minds; [24] and to put
> on the new self, created to be like God in true
> righteousness and holiness.**
>
> **Ephesians 4:22-24**

When we **1.** put off the flesh, **2.** change our thinking, and **3.** learn to live out of our new righteous & holy nature with the help of the Holy Spirit we'll be spirit-controlled rather than flesh-ruled. We'll naturally bear forth fruit of the spirit rather than works of the flesh. This is the key to living according to the Old Testament moral Law. This isn't possible by putting the Law in front of you and trying to force your flesh to conform, which is being "under the law."

First Timothy 1:8-11 goes on to stress that the moral Law was made "for lawbreakers and rebels, the ungodly and sinful, the unholy and irreligious" (verse 9). Paul then provides a list of various sinful lifestyles, like fornicators, sodomites and liars. God's moral Law was "made for" such people in that it reveals to them that they're in sin, which can lead them to the Savior, the gospel, spiritual regeneration and the attainment of righteousness in Christ. At this point they won't need the Law anymore; they'll just need to learn how to put off the "old man" and put on the "new man" because — when they do this — they'll walk in "true righteousness and holiness." Obviously if someone is walking in "true righteousness" they have no need for the Law. This, by the way, explains a mysterious statement Paul made after listing the fruits of the spirit:

> **But the fruit of the Spirit is love, joy peace, patience, kindness, goodness, faithfulness, gentleness and self-control. <u>Against such things there is no law</u>.**
>
> **Galatians 5:22-23**

When believers learn how to live out of their new nature as led of the Holy Spirit they'll be spirit-controlled rather than flesh-ruled and naturally produce the fruit of the spirit, which are the fruits of God's very nature! Such people need no external law to produce these godly attitudes and behaviors! This is why the Bible says that the Law is not for the righteous, but for the unrighteous. The righteous have no need of the Law. Why? Because they're already producing the fruits of righteousness through living out of their spirit by the Holy Spirit. They're spirit-controlled, not flesh-ruled. It's the *un*righteous who need the Law.

This would include believers who may stumble into sin. Say if believers are living in adultery, fornication, homosexuality, lying or strife. We can go to them and show them through God's moral Law that they are in sin and need to repent. **This is how you use the Law lawfully or properly.** Once they humbly repent God forgives them and they are cleansed from "all unrighteousness." At which point they'll no longer need the Law because they're righteous, as this passage clearly shows:

> **If we claim to be without sin, we deceive ourselves and the truth is not in us. If we confess our sins he is faithful and just and will forgive us our sins and purify us from all unrighteousness.**
> **1 John 1:8-9**

As long as believers "keep in repentance" in this manner, as John the Baptist put it (Luke 3:8), they walk in the grace of God's forgiveness and are righteous in Christ because God purifies them "from all unrighteousness" when they humbly confess. If the LORD cleanses believers of *all* unrighteousness, what's that make them? Completely righteous. As such, they have no need of the Law because the Law was made for the unrighteous, not the righteous.

Unsaved People *have* the Moral Law in their Spirit

Speaking of the Law being made for the unrighteous, all unsaved people *have* the moral law, as noted here:

> **Indeed, when <u>Gentiles,</u> <u>who do not have the law,</u>
> do by nature things required by the law, they are
> a law for themselves, even though they do not
> have the law. [15] They show that <u>the requirements</u>
> <u>of the law are written on their hearts,</u> <u>their</u>
> <u>consciences also bearing witness,</u> and their
> thoughts sometimes accusing them and at other
> times even defending them.**
>
>

Romans 2:14-15

Unsaved people were never given the Mosaic Law like the Hebrews were given at Sinai. They're hence ignorant of the ritualistic & kosher laws and understandably so. However, they were given the moral Law at birth in the sense that **it's written in their hearts via the human spirit**, which explains **conscience**. When you were an unbeliever, did you ever feel bad about committing a certain sin? Of course you did. Me too. This is due to conscience. Unfortunately, unregenerate people typically harden their hearts to the voice of their conscience (Ephesians 4:17-19). This means that they close their inner ear to the moral law within and this makes it easier for them to commit the sin in question, which then becomes a justified lifestyle. They desperately need regenerated by the Spirit if they are to effectively live according to the law of love. This is why Christ stressed that all people — Jew and Gentile — need "born again" where the "Spirit gives birth to spirit" (John 3:3,6).

When people are spiritually regenerated in this manner they're reconciled to God, receive eternal life in their spirit and are indwelt by the Holy Spirit, our Helper. They then learn to "participate in the divine nature" (2 Peter 1:4), **which automatically fulfills the moral Law**. This is what the message of Christ is all about and explains why it's such "good news"!

3

—

Why Do Legalists Prefer the Law?

Legalists by definition prefer to focus on religious laws at the expense of living by the spirit. That's why they're called legalists. As shown in the New Testament, the Pharisees and Teachers of the Law were staunch legalists. This spiritual disease has been a huge problem throughout Church history and up to today.

This was the problem Paul was having with the Galatian churches circa 50 AD less than two decades after Christ's death and resurrection. Jewish legalists infiltrated these Gentile fellowships and put them into bondage to various religious laws, like circumcision, strict Sabbath observation, special fasts introduced during the Babylonian captivity, the Jewish feast days and the seven 7-year periods that culminated in the year of Jubilee (Galatians 4:10).

This understandably upset Paul, who was a former Pharisee, especially since he founded all or most of the churches to whom he was writing. Notice what he asks the Galatian believers in exasperation:

You foolish Galatians! <u>Who has</u> <u>bewitched you</u>? Before your very eyes Jesus Christ was clearly portrayed as crucified. [2] I would like to learn just one thing from you: Did you receive the Spirit by observing the law, or by what you heard? [3] Are you so foolish? After beginning with the Spirit, are you now trying to attain your goal by human effort?

Galatians 3:1-3

This so perplexed and grieved Paul that he was led of the Spirit to explain to the Galatians the actual purpose of the Law, concluding with this thought:

So the law was put in charge to lead us to Christ that we might be justified by faith. <u>Now</u> <u>that faith has come,</u> <u>we are no longer under the</u> <u>supervision of the law</u>.

Galatians 3:24-25

Since believers are justified in God's sight by faith **we are no longer under the supervision of the Law**. As noted in chapter <u>1</u>, 'Supervision' is translated as "schoolmaster" in the King James Version. The original Greek word refers to a domestic servant or slave whose business was to train and oversee male youngsters until they came of age at which point the sons took on the duties and liberties of maturity. I'm sure you get the point: Believers are no longer under the supervision of Old Testament Law. Since we are spiritually regenerated and have the Holy Spirit we are liberated to operate in the responsibilities and freedoms of spiritual adulthood, keeping in mind that the Bible shows three stages of

Christian growth — "**children**," "**young men**" (or young women) and "**fathers**" (or mothers) (1 John 2:9-14).[2]

If this is so, why on earth would believers go back to a system of do's and don'ts, like the Galatians started doing? Why would spiritually regenerated believers submit themselves to a former slave — that is, the supervision of the Law — and have "him" oversee them? It's both foolish and absurd, not to mention a denial of the believer's rights as sons and daughters of the Most High!

So why do some do it? Why revert to a system of rules and regulations that can only give the outward appearance of godliness and not the real deal?

One obvious reason is laziness. In some perverted sense it's easier to submit to a system of laws than to think for oneself. You'll see this mentality in Christians who wholly submit their lives to authoritarian pastors/churches that tell them precisely what to do and believe. As such, they don't have to think for themselves; they just follow the authoritarians and their commands or rules.

Other reasons are insecurity and fear. Some believers are so insecure that they need someone to tell them what to do and believe. They're simply not secure in who they are in Christ and, consequently, they're weak. They're afraid of the responsibilities and freedoms that come with spiritual adulthood and therefore never really grow up. It's akin to the security of working for a company all your life rather than deal with the uncertainties of striking out on your own. Although the latter would provide a sense of adventure, freedom and change, the former provides much security and comfort. Why risk the unknown? For these same reasons millions of believers languish in dead fellowships.

Preferring the security of being an employee rather than being your own master is perfectly okay for the labor market, if

---

[2] See the article *Spiritual Growth—The Four Stages* at the Fountain of Life site for details.

that's what a person prefers, but it's unhealthy in the realm of the spirit. There are plenty of legalists, libertines and authoritarians out there who are more than willing to take advantage of believers who refuse to take the reins of spiritual growth and maturity.

Since legalists refuse to foster an actual relationship with the LORD they have no choice but to divert to rules and regulations. This isn't to say they won't go through the motions of having a relationship, but this is chiefly for appearances sake. In some cases they may actually pray in their private time, but it's very rehearsed, one-sided and lifeless, like talking to a wall. They likely do this to convince themselves that they actually have a relationship with God. If your prayer time is dry, one-dimensional and boring, take note. Legalism is creeping in.

Lastly, in addition to lacking an actual relationship with the Lord, legalistic leaders prefer religious rules so they can dominate others and foster a dependent following of sheeple. Such dependency naturally feeds the leaders' egos.

4

Legalists Focus on Rules above Relationship

The gospel is referred to as the "message of reconciliation" in Scripture (2 Corinthians 5:17-21). Why? Because it is through the good news of the gospel that people are *reconciled* with their Creator. 'Reconciliation' means "to turn from enmity to friendship" and this is the core of the Christian message: We can have an actual relationship with God through spiritual regeneration via the imperishable seed of the enduring Word of God, Jesus Christ (1 Peter 1:23 & 1 John 3:9). I should add that 'seed' in the Greek is "sperm" (in the latter verse) — we've been born-again of the imperishable *sperm* of Christ, the Living Word of God.

Since legalism is the definition of hypocrisy — that is, putting on an act — legalists can't stress relationship; consequently, they divert to religious rules, including the many rules they make up. Why do they dream up new rules or laws? Because they're obsessed with them, *that's* legal-ism.

While this brief chapter is somewhat off-topic and you're welcome to jump ahead to the next one, I think it's important to establish how legalists veer from *relationship* with the LORD to focus on *rules*.

Notice what Jesus said about the legalists of the 1st century:

> " 'These people honor me with their lips,
>   but their hearts are far from me.
> [7] They worship me in vain;
>   their teachings are but rules taught by men.'
>
> [8] You have let go of the command of God and are holding on to the traditions of men..."
> [13] "Thus you nullify the word of God by your tradition that you have handed down."
>
> **Mark 7:6-8 & 13**

What we see here is a tendency of legalists to dream up rules that go beyond Scripture. The Bible is full of moral commands, which can be condensed into the two greatest commands with three applications: loving God and loving people as you love yourself (Matthew 22:34-40). But this isn't good enough for legalists; they have to add more rules. Paul commented on this fleshly tendency when he wrote to the Colossians:

> **Since you died with Christ to the basic principles of this world, why, as though you still belonged to it, do you submit to its rules: [21] "Do not handle! Do not taste! Do not touch!"? [22] These are destined to perish with use, because they are based on human commands and teachings. [23] Such regulations indeed have an appearance of wisdom with their self-imposed worship, their false humility and their harsh**

treatment of the body, but <u>they lack any value in restraining sensual indulgence.</u>
Colossians 2:20-23

Notice Paul is denouncing human commands and teachings, not biblical ones rooted in faith & love. Such rules only have an appearance of wisdom and have no real power to restrain carnality (verse 23). Only spiritual rebirth, renewing the mind and putting off the old self / putting on the new self, provide the power to walk in true righteousness and holiness (Ephesians 4:22-24).

Also observe in verse 21 how Paul literally mocks the goofy rules that legalists dream up: "Do not handle! Do not taste! Do not touch!" *He's making fun of their stupid rules!* **Notice that one of the rules he mocks is "Do not taste!"**

Legalists do the same thing today as they did in the 1st century. Here are ten modern examples:

- **"Don't drink caffeinated beverages"**
- **"Don't drink alcoholic beverages"**
- **"Don't eat pork or meat?"**
- **"King James only!"**
- **"You're only welcome at our church services if adorned in dress clothes"** otherwise known as **"Suit and tie only!"**
- **"You can celebrate this and that holiday but not this or that holiday"**
- **"You must not view an R-rated movie"**
- **"You can't play competitive games, like football, including board games, like chess"**
- **"Marital couples can only have sex in the missionary position; all other sexual expressions are forbidden"**
- **"You must witness door-to-door or you're not a true believer"**

Eye-rolling rules like these bring to mind Jesus' potent observation about legalists: "They worship me in vain; **their teachings are but rules taught by men**" (Mark 7:7). For details proving why these kinds of rules are irrelevant to the believer see Chapter 2 of *Legalism Unmasked*.[3]

While extra-biblical rules that religious people dream up are technically outside of this book's topic, I wanted to show how legalists reject relationship with God in preference for rules.

---

[3] Or see the article *Legalism — Understanding its Many Forms* at the Fountain of Life site.

5
—

What about Dietary & Ceremonial Laws?

The New Testament believer is free of the ceremonial and dietary laws of the old covenant and are only obligated to fulfill the moral law, which we do by walking in the spirit — i.e. "participating in the divine nature" (2 Peter 1:4) — and not by putting ourselves under the Law, as detailed in chapter 1. That believers are required to fulfill the moral law but not the ceremonial & dietary laws can be observed by the fact that Old Testament moral laws are cited in the New Testament (e.g. Luke 4:8 & Acts 23:5), but never the ceremonial or dietary laws, including Sabbath-keeping. As a matter of fact, notice what the Word of God blatantly says on the matter:

> **When you were dead in your sins and in the uncircumcision of your flesh, God made you alive with Christ. He forgave us all our sins, [14] having canceled the charge of our legal indebtedness, which stood against us and condemned us; he has taken it away, nailing it to**

the cross. [15] **And having disarmed the powers
and authorities, he made a public spectacle of
them, triumphing over them by the cross.**

[16] **<u>Therefore</u> do not let anyone judge you
by <u>what you eat</u> or <u>drink</u>, or with regard to <u>a
religious festival</u>, a <u>New Moon celebration</u> or <u>a
Sabbath day</u>. [17] <u>These are a shadow of the things
that were to come</u>; <u>the reality</u>, however, <u>is found
in Christ</u>.**

Colossians 2:13-17

Christ came to fulfill the righteous requirements of the Law
on our behalf (Matthew 5:17) and, in fact, he is the "culmination of
the law" — the "end of the law" — "so that there may be
righteousness for everyone who believes" (Romans 10:4). As
detailed in chapters 1 and 2, "everyone who believes" attains
righteousness through spiritual rebirth (2 Corinthians 5:21) and
then learning to live out of his/her new nature with the help of the
Holy Spirit. The reason this works is because the believer's
regenerated spirit is the "new self," which is "created to be *like
God* in **true righteousness** and **holiness**" (Ephesians 4:22-24). As
such, learning to put off the flesh — the sin nature — and put on
the new self — our godly nature — is the key to fulfilling the
moral law. The Holy Spirit is *in* us to help do this, which is why
the Spirit is called our "helper" (John 14:26[4]). Those who are led
of the Spirit in this manner "are not under the law" (Galatians
5:18).

I realize I'm repeating data from previous chapters here,
but this material is mandatory for believers to walk in newness of
life (Romans 6:4). Master these scriptural axioms and you will
walk free of the flesh and legal-ism; you'll soar in the spirit!

Notice again what God's Word says:

---

[4] ESV, NASB, ISV, Good News Translation, Berean Literal Bible and several more.

> **Therefore do not let anyone judge you by
> what you eat or drink, or with regard to a
> religious festival, a New Moon celebration or a
> Sabbath day. [17] These are a shadow of the things
> that were to come; the reality, however, is found
> in Christ.**
>
> **Colossians 2:16-17**

The passage is addressing the dietary and ceremonial laws of the Old Testament: "what you eat or drink" refers to dietary laws and the others refer to ritualistic laws. We are not to allow legalists to judge us negatively by these things. In fact, all of them — kosher laws, the Jewish festivals, the New Moon celebration and the Sabbath day — **are a mere shadow of what was to come, meaning Jesus Christ, the Anointed One**. "The reality is found in Christ" and if you're a believer YOU are "in Christ."

Everything in the law and prophets from Genesis to Malachi were types and shadows of the true reality, which is Christ and the spiritual rebirth that comes through his seed (sperm), not to mention the power of the Holy Spirit, who indwells, helps and guides the believer. More than 600 laws were given to the Hebrews in the Old Testament and Jesus fulfilled every one of them; he completed or stopped every one of them, including the Sabbath.

All Foods are Declared Clean in the New Testament

It always surprises me — even shocks me — when I come across believers who staunchly advocate that Christians should obey the Old Testament dietary laws. Why? Because it's so absolutely clear in the Bible that believers are liberated from these laws in the New Testament era, the age of grace. Let's start with what Christ himself clearly taught on the issue:

> **"Are you so dull? Don't you see that <u>nothing that</u> <u>enters a person from the outside can defile them</u>? ¹⁹ For it doesn't go into their heart but into their stomach, and then out of the body." (<u>In saying</u> <u>this, Jesus declared all foods clean</u>.)"**
>
> **Mark 7:18-19**

As you can see, no food that enters a person from the outside can defile them! (Please understand that the Lord was talking about any & all legitimate *foods* here). The passage goes on to matter-of-factly state that "Jesus declared all foods clean." If language means anything we have to conclude that the Lord, in fact, declared all foods clean.

Is this backed-up by the rest of the New Testament? Absolutely. Let's start with Peter's vision of a sheet of unclean animals let down from heaven:

> **Then a voice told him, "Get up, Peter. <u>Kill and</u> <u>eat</u>."**
>
> **"Surely not, Lord!" Peter replied. "I have never eaten anything impure or unclean."**
>
> **The voice spoke to him a second time, "Do not call anything impure <u>that God has made</u> <u>clean</u>..."**
>
> **This happened three times, and immediately the sheet was taken back to heaven.**
>
> **Acts 10:13-16 & 11:7-10**

As you can see, this passage appears twice in the New Testament verbatim and corresponds to what Jesus said above. Why does it appear twice verbatim? Because the LORD is trying to get something across to us and wants to make sure that we get it.

Now legalists will argue that the purpose of the vision had nothing to do with food and everything to do with God granting salvation to those considered unclean by Jews — the Gentiles — as shown in Acts 11:18. Actually, **the vision applied to food literally and to the Gentiles figuratively**. Why else would the Lord give Peter a vision of unclean animals and proceed to declare them clean *three times* and then have the account repeated verbatim *twice* in the book of Acts? If the Lord was only talking about Gentiles being declared clean in Christ, why use the vision of unclean animals at all? Why say "Kill and eat" if he was only referring to people? (Unless, of course, God wants us to become cannibals). Why not just have a sheet of Gentile folks appear to Peter wherein the Lords says, "Do not call anything impure that God has made clean"? The obvious answer is that the vision applied to *both*, especially when you consider what Jesus already said about all foods being declared clean (Mark 7:19), not to mention what the epistles consistently teach about the believer's dietary intake.

Let's look at these verses:

> **One person's faith allows them to <u>eat anything</u>, but another, whose faith is weak, <u>eats only vegetables</u>.**
> **Romans 14:2**

> **I am convinced, being fully persuaded <u>in the Lord Jesus</u>, that <u>nothing is unclean in itself</u>. But if anyone regards something as unclean, then for that person it is unclean. [15] If your brother or sister is distressed because of what you eat, you are no longer acting in love. Do not by your eating destroy someone for whom Christ died.**
> **Romans 14:14-15**

For <u>the kingdom of God is not a matter of eating</u> <u>and drinking, but of righteousness</u>, peace and joy in the Holy Spirit.

Romans 14:17

Do not destroy the work of God for the sake of food. <u>All food is clean</u>, but it is wrong for a person to eat anything that causes someone else to stumble.

Romans 14:20

But <u>food does not bring us near to God</u>; we are no worse if we do not eat, and no better if we do.

1 Corinthians 8:8

Therefore do not let anyone judge you by <u>what you eat or drink</u>

Colossians 2:16

The Spirit clearly says that in later times some <u>will abandon the faith</u> and <u>follow deceiving</u> <u>spirits and things taught by demons.</u> [2] Such teachings come through hypocritical liars, whose consciences have been seared as with a hot iron. [3] They forbid people to marry and order them to <u>abstain from certain foods,</u> <u>which God created to</u> <u>be received with thanksgiving by those who</u> <u>believe and who know the truth.</u> [4] <u>For everything</u> <u>God created is good, and nothing is to be</u> <u>rejected if it is received with thanksgiving,</u> [5] because it is consecrated by the word of God and prayer.

1 Timothy 4:1-5

THE LAW and the Believer

Do not be carried away by all kinds of strange teachings. It is good for our hearts to be strengthened by grace, <u>not by eating ceremonial foods</u>, <u>which is of no benefit to those who do so</u>.
Hebrews 13:9

In addition, Paul gave this instruction to Gentile believers in a Gentile city:

<u>Eat</u> <u>anything</u> <u>sold in the meat market</u> without raising questions of conscience, ²⁶ <u>for</u>, "The earth is the Lord's, <u>and everything in it</u>."
1 Corinthians 10:25-26

These passages couldn't be any clearer that all foods are declared clean in the New Testament period and that the kingdom of God is not about eating and drinking because, as Paul says, "food does not bring us near to God; we are no worse if we do not eat, and no better if we do." Christ expressed the same thought when he said, "Are you so dull? Don't you see that nothing that enters a person from the outside can defile them?" (Mark 7:18). In other words, it's just common sense that food doesn't have the capacity to harm us spiritually.

Whether a believer chooses to have shrimp for supper or some bacon for breakfast doesn't mean anything in the kingdom of God, as long as **1. we're not gluttons** — that is, we don't make an idol of food — and **2. we do all things in moderation** (1 Corinthians 6:12 & 10:23). After all, too much of *anything* isn't good. Of course, certain foods are known to be problematic health-wise and so it's just wise to limit your intake of them, like bacon.

It's also prudent to limit your exposure to dubious foods for which you have a weakness. I *love* Dorito chips, vanilla ice cream, egg nog and soy milk and it's for this very reason that Carol & I don't allow these items in our household too often. Yes, I realize soy milk is healthy, but I tend to drink too much of it and — again — too much of *anything* isn't good.

Notice how 1 Timothy 4:1-5 shows that false teachers will rise up and follow deceiving spirits and one of their false doctrines will be instructing people to "abstain from certain foods, which God created to be received with thanksgiving for those who believe… For everything God created is good, and nothing is to be rejected if it is received with thanksgiving."

If words mean anything we have no recourse but to conclude that all foods are declared clean for the believer! Be on your guard against so-called Christians & groups who insist on obedience to Old Testament dietary laws and abstaining from certain foods, like meat. You can be sure that such people are following deceiving spirits who want to get believers back *under* the Law where there's no life: "For the letter kills, but the Spirit gives life" (2 Corinthians 3:6).

We'll examine several arguments for obeying Old Covenant kosher laws in chapter **11**.

6

The Issue of Circumcision

The apostle Paul knew how to recognize legalists because he used to be one. Notice how he refers to legalists in this passage:

> **Beware of the <u>dogs</u>, beware of the <u>evil workers</u>, beware of those <u>who mutilate the flesh</u>! For it is we who are the circumcision, who worship in the Spirit of God and boast in Christ Jesus and have no confidence in the flesh.**
> **Philippians 3:2-3** (NRSV)

Paul was warning the Philippian believers of legalists who taught that non-Jews had to be physically circumcised in order to be truly saved. They were obsessed with it. Notice that Paul doesn't mince words here. He blatantly calls these legalists "dogs" and "evil workers"!

Calling someone a "dog" was even more offensive in biblical times than it is today. The term referred to people of low moral character. For instance, "dogs" is used in the Bible in reference to homosexual prostitutes (Deuteronomy 23:18), wicked betrayers (Psalm 59:5-6), corrupt leaders (Isaiah 56:10), heathen people (Matthew 15:26-27) and, in this passage, staunch legalists.

How would you like to be called an "evil worker"? That's pretty harsh, don't you agree? This is recorded in God's Word to show us that legalism is utter wickedness in the LORD's eyes. It cannot be tolerated; it must be confronted, exposed and reproved. And believers need to be warned for their protection.

Roughly a decade earlier, the Judaizers corrupted the churches in Galatia with a "different gospel" (Galatians 1:6), a gospel mixed with Jewish law. Paul said the Galatian believers were "bewitched" for tolerating this heresy and allowing it to corrupt their assemblies (Galatians 3:1). Notice what he blatantly says about these legalists:

> **If anybody is preaching to you a gospel other than what you accepted, <u>let him be eternally condemned</u>!**
>
> **Galatians 1:9**

Paul says that anyone who preached this different gospel should "be eternally condemned!" You know what this means in plain English? "Let 'em go to hell!" Yes, as unbelievable as it may seem, Paul, the greatest figure of Christianity after Jesus Christ, forcefully declared that those who *unrepentantly* preached a different gospel — a "gospel" which soiled the body of Christ with legalism — should be forever damned!

Needless to say, legalism is a grievous sin in God's eyes and cannot be tolerated, whether in myself, yourself or others. It must be recognized, corrected and purged ASAP.

As noted in chapter 1, this "different gospel" included the practice of circumcision, the cutting off of the male foreskin, which was commanded in the Torah:

On the eighth day the boy is to be circumcised.
Leviticus 12:3

But physical circumcision is *not* necessary in the new covenant because believers are circumcised inwardly through spiritual regeneration (Romans 2:29 & Titus 3:5). As such, this is what Paul told the Galatian believers about circumcision:

> **Mark my words! I, Paul, tell you that <u>if</u> <u>you let yourselves be circumcised, Christ will be</u> <u>of no value to you at all</u>. [3] Again I declare to every man who lets himself be circumcised that he is obligated to obey the whole law. [4] <u>You who</u> <u>are trying to be justified by the law have been</u> <u>alienated from Christ; you have fallen away</u> <u>from grace</u>. [5] For through the Spirit we eagerly await by faith the righteousness for which we hope. [6] <u>For in Christ Jesus neither circumcision</u> <u>nor uncircumcision has any value</u>. The only thing that counts is <u>faith expressing itself</u> <u>through love</u>.**
>
> **Galatians 5:2-6**

Paul blatantly warns the Galatians that, if they allowed themselves to be circumcised, Christ would be of no use to them at all! He equates any attempt to be justified by the Law — including the practice of circumcision — to being "alienated from Christ" and "fallen away from grace." Lastly, he points out in verse 6 that whether someone's physically circumcised or not holds no value for those "in Christ Jesus," meaning believers.

Numerous other New Testament passages teach against the practice of circumcision in relation to the Mosaic Law, including: Acts 15, 1 Corinthians 7:17-20, Galatians 2:1-3, Galatians 6:12-16, Philippians 3:2-3, Colossians 2:11, 3:11 and Titus 1:10.

This is a crushing blow to the arguments of legalists who try to add one element of the Law or another to faith in Christ. How so? Because circumcision was clearly part of the Torah — the Old Testament Law — and the New Testament plainly says that it is not applicable to New Testament believers, just like Sabbath-keeping, observing the feast days and dietary laws. These things were but a shadow of what was to come, the reality is found in Christ (Colossians 2:16-17).

I should add that Paul had his missionary helper circumcised, but this was so that Timothy wouldn't hinder the spread of the gospel as they reached out to unsaved Jews (Acts 16:1-3). This was in line with Paul's missionary strategy, which he put like this: "Though I am free and belong to no one, I have made myself a slave to everyone, to win as many as possible. **To the Jews I became like a Jew, to win the Jews.** To those under the law I became *like* one under the law (though I myself am not under the law), so as to win those under the law" (1 Corinthians 9:19-20).

Circumcision was the Sign of the Abrahamic Covenant

We first hear of circumcision in the Bible as a sign of the covenant God made with Abraham through faith. This contract promised that the LORD would make Abraham "the father of many nations" — meaning he would have countless descendants — and that the land of Canaan would be theirs forever (Genesis 17:3-8). More importantly, God promised that all peoples on earth would be blessed through one of Abraham's descendants, which referred to the Messiah (Genesis 12:1-3,7 & Galatians 3:16). The outward sign of this agreement was circumcision for Abraham and all his descendants (Genesis 17:9–14 & Acts 7:8). It might help to grasp the concept of an outward sign of a covenant by considering our marriage contract and the corresponding wedding rings.

Four hundred years later, Abraham's descendants were groaning as slaves in Egypt and cried out to God. Thus the LORD "remembered **his covenant with Abraham**" (Exodus 2:24) and — being faithful to this agreement — delivered the Hebrews from Egypt and began to lead them to the land he promised their forefather.

During their journey to the Promised Land the Israelites entered into an additional covenant with God, which was the Mosaic Covenant (Exodus 19-20 & 24:7-8). Like the Abrahamic Covenant, this covenant required an outward sign, which was Sabbath-keeping (Exodus 31:12).

The Sabbath day Law was one of the Ten Commandments (Exodus 20). The Ten Commandments were inscribed on two stone tablets and they **embodied the entire Mosaic Covenant**, which is why they're referred to as "the words of the covenant" and "the tablets of the covenant" (Exodus 34:28 & Deuteronomy 9:9). In other words, the Ten Commandments represented the whole of the Law (Torah) of which there were over 600 laws.

When this covenant was made at Mt. Sinai, **the Israelites were under two covenants**: The Abrahamic Covenant with its sign of circumcision and the Mosaic Covenant with its sign of Sabbath observance.

Three things need stressed: **1.** The promise of a redeemer of the world came though the Abrahamic Covenant and this was much more important than the Mosaic Covenant; **2.** the Mosaic Law was "added because of transgression until the Seed to whom the promise referred had come" (Galatians 3:19), which indicates that **3.** the Covenant of the Law would expire when the Abrahamic Covenant was fulfilled in Christ. This means that the Mosaic Covenant was a temporary contract.

We clearly observe these points here:

¹⁶ The promises were spoken to Abraham and to his seed. Scripture does not say "and to seeds," meaning many people, but "and to your seed," meaning one person, who is <u>Christ</u>. ¹⁷ What I mean is this: The law, introduced 430 years later, does not set aside the covenant previously established by God and thus do away with the promise. ¹⁸ For if the inheritance depends on the law, then it no longer depends on the promise; but God in his grace gave it to Abraham through a promise.

¹⁹ <u>Why, then, was the law given at all? It was added because of transgressions until the Seed to whom the promise referred had come.</u> The law was given through angels and entrusted to a mediator.

Galatians 3:16-19

Verse 16 shows that the future "seed" promised to Abraham ultimately referred to Christ, our Redeemer. And verse 17 points out that the Mosaic Covenant given 430 years later did not cancel out the Abrahamic Covenant.

Verse 19 then reveals **1.** *WHY* the Law was added and **2.** that it would only be relevant "until" that Seed had come, meaning Christ. In other words, **the Mosaic Covenant of the Law had an expiration date!** And that expiration date was the coming of Christ.

Paul goes on to elaborate:

Before the coming of this faith, we were held in custody under the law, locked up until the faith that was to come would be revealed. ²⁴ So the law was our guardian <u>until</u> Christ came that we might be justified by faith. ²⁵ <u>Now that</u>

this faith has come, we are no longer under a guardian.

Galatians 3:23-25

The Law is defined as a "guardian **until** Christ came." Ever since Christ came we are "no longer under that guardian." Could God's Word be any clearer? To suggest that New Covenant believers are still under the Mosaic Law shouldn't even be a consideration.

Our conclusion on circumcision is that this practice was an outward sign of the Abrahamic Covenant and a law of the Mosaic Covenant. The former *promised* Christ while the latter *pointed to* Christ. Ever since Jesus came and completed his mission as Redeemer of the world the practice of circumcision has become irrelevant. New Covenant believers — male *and* female — receive an **inward circumcision** through spiritual regeneration (Romans 2:29 & Titus 3:5).

7

—

Should Believers Observe the Sabbath?

The first question we want to answer here is: What is the Sabbath? Then we'll consider if New Covenant believers are obligated to observe it; and — if so — in what capacity?

There are some misconceptions about the Sabbath, so let's read God's specific instructions to the Israelites on this issue:

"Remember the Sabbath day by keeping it holy.
[9] Six days you shall labor and do all your
work, [10] but the seventh day is a sabbath to
the Lord your God. On it <u>you shall not do</u>
<u>any work</u>, neither you, nor your son or
daughter, nor your male or female servant,
nor your animals, nor any foreigner residing
in your towns. [11] For in six days the Lord
made the heavens and the earth, the sea, and

all that is in them, but he <u>rested</u> on the seventh day. Therefore the Lord blessed the Sabbath day and made it holy."

Exodus 20:8-11

The Hebrew word for Sabbath is *shabath (shaw-BATH)*, which means to "cease" or "desist from labor." It simply means to "rest." This can be seen in the first appearance of the word in Scripture:

Then God blessed the seventh day and made it holy, because on it he <u>rested</u> *(shabath)* from all the work of creating that he had done.

Genesis 2:3

To make something holy means to set it apart from the mundane. So designating the seventh day as "holy" simply means **to set it apart** from the other six days of the week as **a day of rest**. So when the LORD much later established the Sabbath for the Israelites in the Law — as shown above — it was simply as a day of rest from one's labor, that's it.

While it's presumed that a person celebrating the Sabbath would naturally worship the LORD there's nothing in this particular passage that says people have to meet on that day to worship together, although Leviticus 23:3 throws in this additional element where "sacred assembly" refers to the community being summoned together for common worship **and celebration**. Yet meeting with other people and worshipping together is not the essence of the command, but rather resting from one's labors, which presupposes honoring God and celebration. When you have a break from your job (or school), what do you automatically do? Give thanks and celebrate in one way or another, right? This would likely include getting together with family & friends. It's the same principle.

The LORD commanded the Israelites to observe the Sabbath for all generations as a sign of the lasting covenant between God and them (Exodus 31:16-17). It was meant to be a blessing to the Israelites — a day to rest, celebrate and refresh — but, by the time of Christ, sourpuss legalists had largely turned it into a burden. These religionists became so technical about defining what "work" was and wasn't that they came up with myriad rules, like the "Sabbath Day's journey," which was less than half-a-mile, the distance Israelites were allowed to travel on the Sabbath without violating it (Acts 1:12).

The Pharisees are the quintessential example of legalism in the Bible, which can be seen in their objections to Jesus' mere intention of healing a man's deformed hand on the Sabbath, as shown here:

> **Another time Jesus went into the synagogue, and a man with a shriveled hand was there. ² Some of them were looking for a reason to accuse Jesus, so they watched him closely to see if he would heal him on the Sabbath. ³ Jesus said to the man with the shriveled hand, "Stand up in front of everyone."**
>
> **⁴ Then Jesus asked them, "Which is lawful on the Sabbath: to do good or to do evil, to save life or to kill?" But they remained silent.**
>
> **⁵ He looked around at them in anger and, deeply distressed at their stubborn hearts, said to the man, "Stretch out your hand." He stretched it out, and his hand was completely restored. ⁶ Then the Pharisees went out and began to plot with the Herodians how they might kill Jesus.**
>
> **Mark 3:1-6**

The Pharisees were so ridiculously detailed and rigid with their rules concerning "working" on the Sabbath that they opposed Jesus doing any type of healing "work" on that day. Christ was so disgusted by their stubbornness that he shot them all a glance of anger, as shown in verse 5. This was righteous anger, of course, but anger nevertheless. He then proceeded to heal the man despite their legalistic objections. This was a wordless reprimand to them; and they were so offended that they decided to murder him!

Can you imagine people being so blinded by legalistic zeal that they object to an incredible healing? Make no mistake, this is what the poison of legalism does when people are seriously infected. Those who are not contaminated, by contrast, are ever ready to praise God when others are miraculously healed and set free. Take, for instance, the occasion when blind Bartimaeus received his sight through faith and he immediately glorified God. The passage goes on to say, "And all the people, when they saw it, gave praise to God" (Luke 18:43 NKJV). This is how *normal* people react to incredible healings and life-changing miracles. Not so with legalists. They're so preoccupied and corrupted by rule-ism they can't see the forest for the trees!

On another occasion the Messiah and his disciples were walking through the fields on the Sabbath and picked some heads of grain to quell their hunger. Since it was the Sabbath the Pharisees argued that the disciples were guilty of working because they plucked the grain and rubbed it in their hands before eating. To their legalistic way of thinking this was equal to reaping and threshing. The Mosaic Law did forbid working on the Sabbath but it was intended to be a blessing, not a burden. The Sabbath was supposed to be a welcomed rest and celebration after a 6-day work week, not a joyless ritual observing man-made technicalities. Jesus' simple-yet-brilliant response says it all:

> "The Sabbath was made for man, not man for the Sabbath."
>
> Mark 2:27[5]

God's Commands are NOT Burdensome

God is always interested in blessing people by setting them free while religionists are intent on burdening others and putting them into spiritual bondage. Notice what Jesus said of the Teachers of the Law and the Pharisees: "They tie up heavy loads and put them on men's shoulders, but they themselves are not willing to lift a finger to move them" (Matthew 23:4). By contrast, the Bible says:

> **This is love for God: to obey his commands. <u>And his commands are not burdensome</u>, for everyone born of God overcomes the world. This is the victory that has overcome the world, even our <u>faith</u>.**
>
> **1 John 5:3-4**

All of God's moral laws in the Old Testament can be condensed into two basic commands with three applications: **Love God** and **love people** as you **love yourself**. That's it. And these commands are not burdensome because believers are born of God and have the spiritual nature to joyfully fulfill them with the help of the Spirit. The only believers who have trouble doing this are those who fail to put off the flesh and are therefore flesh-ruled. As such, the "law of sin and death" is at work in their lives and this is no fun because sin's reward is death. But those who walk in the spirit are spirit-controlled and therefore the "law of the spirit of

---

[5] You can compare the three accounts of this occasion as shown in Matthew 12:1-8, Mark 2:23-28 and Luke 6:1-5.

life" is in motion, which is a higher law than the law of sin and death (Romans 8:2).

Did you ever marvel at how huge aircrafts are able to defy the law of gravity and soar above the landscape? How do they do this? It's simple: They activate a higher law, the law of lift and propulsion, which neutralizes the law of gravity. As long as the higher law is in motion the lower law is rendered powerless. Just as the physical law of lift and propulsion enables people to conquer gravity and fly, so the law of the spirit of life — when it is in motion — deactivates the law of sin and death. This is "walking in the spirit" or "participating in the divine nature." Such a law is not burdensome, but man-made religion is.[6]

Observe what Christ said about God's commands not being burdensome in the kingdom of God:

> **"Come to me, all you who are weary and burdened, and I will give you rest. Take my yoke upon you and learn from me, for I am gentle and humble in heart and you will find rest for your souls. For my yoke is easy and my burden is light."**
>
> **Matthew 11:28-30**

While religion and the corresponding rule-ism will weigh you down and make you weary, Jesus Christ gives you **rest**. This is the difference between religion and relationship with God. Yes, there is a yoke and burden to serving the Lord but, unlike the yoke of the flesh or the burden of religion, Jesus' yoke is easy and his burden is light. How so? Because that's the nature of the law of love; and love is the fulfillment of the Law (Romans 13:8-10).

---

[6] See the Fountain of Life article *Spirituality—How to be Spirit-Controlled Rather than Flesh-Ruled* and the corresponding video *How to Walk FREE of the Flesh* for details.

The Sabbath and the Believer's Freedom

Getting back to the issue of the Sabbath, someone might argue, "If loving God is to obey God's commands according to 1 John 5:3, then we should love God by obeying his Sabbath command." Answer: The Ten Commandments were just 10 of 613 Old Testament laws; you could say that the Ten Commandments were a starting point for Israel because a lot of important moral commands are glaringly missing from the Ten Commandments, such as do not fornicate, do not commit homosexuality, do not attempt to contact the dead, do not engage in witchcraft, and so on. I've come across Christians who defend, say, fornication on that grounds that "it's not in the top ten," yet — again — The Ten Commandments are just 10 of over 600 laws contained in the Old Testament Law (Torah).

God's instruction to rest on the seventh day wasn't a moral command, but rather a ceremonial one; and believers are not under the ceremonial & dietary laws of the Old Testament. Notice what the New Testament says about this:

> Therefore **do not let anyone judge you by what you eat or drink, or with regard to a religious festival, a New Moon celebration or a Sabbath day.** [17] **These are a shadow of the things that were to come**; the **reality**, however, **is found in Christ**.
>
> **Colossians 2:16-17**

The Sabbath was a shadow of what was to come — Jesus Christ! You must get a hold of this. The dietary laws, feast days and holy days that God commanded in the Old Testament — including the Sabbath — pictured the person and work of the coming Messiah. Jesus carried out all these types through his ministry. Thus the need to observe them has ceased.

THE LAW and the Believer

For the believer there is freedom on the issue, notice:

> **One person considers one day more sacred than another; <u>another considers every day alike</u>. Each of them should be fully convinced in their own mind. ⁶ Whoever regards one day as special does so to the Lord.**
>
> **Romans 14:5-6**

Paul goes on to say: "Therefore let us stop passing judgment on one another. Instead, make up your mind not to put any stumbling block or obstacle in the way of a brother or sister" (Romans 14:13) and earlier he stressed, "Who are you to judge someone else's servant? To their own master, servants stand or fall" (Romans 14:4). So believers have freedom on the issue, but some are more conscious of their freedom than others and, as such, we need to be sensitive and respectful so as not to harm our brother and sister in the Lord.

In the early days of the Church, believers were predominantly Jewish. Antioch was about 500 miles north of Jerusalem (in what is now Turkey) and was the location of the first non-Jewish church, which included some Hebrew believers. There were more Gentile fellowships in Syria and Cilicia. The Jerusalem assembly faced a dilemma, what aspects of the Mosaic Law would the Jewish believers impose on the Gentile believers? Notice what they decided:

> **"It is my judgment, therefore, that we should not make it difficult for the Gentiles who are turning to God. ²⁰ Instead we should write to them, telling them to abstain from food polluted by idols, from sexual immorality, from the meat of strangled animals and from blood."**
>
> **Acts 15:19-20**

Notice that there was **no instruction for the Gentiles to keep the Sabbath or observe the Jewish festivals or celebrate the New Moon, nor to follow the Old Testament dietary laws**. These Messianic Jewish leaders decided it wasn't right to impose Old Testament ceremonial & dietary laws on Gentile believers.

It should be emphasized that this four-item list had nothing to do with God's grace of salvation, which the council had already settled came through faith alone (Acts 15:6-11). However, the list had everything to do with how the Gentile believers could live and worship *with* Jewish believers who were particularly offended by these four types of behaviors and, as such, these four prohibitions were intended to maintain peace and unity in the Gentile churches. Because the Greek and Roman world was filled with pagan religions the council's instructions were focused on helping the Gentile believers to break from their pagan past and ease the consciences of sensitive Hebrew believers in their midst. Hence, the instructions were about the Gentiles cutting themselves off from anything related to pagan worship. They were therefore encouraged not to eat food sacrificed to idols or to participate in pagan festivals, which were marked by all-around sensual revelry, including sexual immorality. Antioch was located in a pagan nation where immorality was rampant.

Several years after this occasion Paul declared eating meat sacrificed to idols acceptable for believers with strong consciences —that is, mature believers — but he stressed that such Christians should remain sensitive to their brothers and sisters with weak consciences who felt eating such meat was intrinsically wrong (1 Corinthians 8). This instruction revealed both the believer's freedom and responsibility. Believers have the liberty to eat such meat but they were also responsible to make sure that the practice of their freedom didn't harm someone with a weak conscience. This is true today with many issues, like drinking alcohol (which is different than being a drunkard) or watching movies or going to a secular concert. Paul stressed, "Be careful... that the exercise of your rights does not become a stumbling block to the weak" (1 Corinthians 8:9).

The point is that **the Jerusalem council did not require Gentile churches to keep the Sabbath**.

So when did early Christians meet and worship together? Read what the Bible says:

> **<u>Every day they continued to meet together in the temple courts</u>. They broke bread <u>in their homes</u> and ate together with glad and sincere hearts, [47] praising God and enjoying the favor of all the people. And the Lord added to their number daily those who were being saved.**
>
> **Acts 2:46-47**

They met together every day at the temple courts and in their homes. If there was a day that Christians met regularly it was the first day of the week, which is our Sunday (Acts 20:7 & 1 Corinthians 16:2). This was in honor of Christ's resurrection on Sunday and should not be viewed as a "Christian Sabbath" but simply as a day to *especially* honor Jesus Christ. Notice what the Bible instructs about New Testament believers meeting together:

> **And let us consider how we may spur one another on toward love and good deeds, [25] <u>not giving up meeting together</u>, as some are in the habit of doing, but encouraging one another— and all the more as you see the Day approaching.**
>
> **Hebrews 10:24-25**

Notice that nothing is said about meeting and worshipping on a *certain* day. Why? Because it's not important. What was important was that they met together. True worship is a lifestyle and a heart attitude; the Messiah said we are to worship "in spirit and truth" (John 4:24). As such, we should practice the presence of Christ 24 hours a day, seven days a week. Not only is there no correct day to worship the Lord, we should worship every day!

Again, Sabbath means "rest" or to "cease from labor." In the New Testament age of grace we are to cease from working for righteousness. Jesus said that we are to come to him because he is our rest, our Sabbath (Matthew 11:28-30). Through Christ we are born righteous in our spirits and, as such, we are already righteous and in-right-standing with God. Of course genuine faith produces works (James 2:14-16), but these works are a result of being righteous and not an attempt to become righteous. Are you following?

The Church is to Rest in Christ's Already Accomplished Work of Salvation

Why did New Testament believers — the Church (literally the "called-out ones") — gather on the first day of the week as shown in Acts 20:7 and 1 Corinthians 16:2? Because the body of Christ is a new creation, and it's very existence was birthed via resting in Christ's already accomplished work of salvation:

> **for anyone who enters <u>God's rest</u> also rests from their works, just as God did from his.**
> **Hebrews 4:10**

New Covenant believers cease performing our own works and the works of the Law, including the Ten Commandments. Instead of working toward victory we work from Christ's already accomplished victory. Let's revisit a key passage with the addition of the preceding two verses:

14 **having canceled the charge of our legal indebtedness, which stood against us and condemned us; he has taken it away, nailing it to the cross. 15 And having disarmed the powers and authorities, he made a public spectacle of them, triumphing over them by the cross.**

16 Therefore <u>do not let anyone judge you by what you eat or drink, or with regard to a religious festival, a New Moon celebration or a Sabbath day</u>. 17 These are <u>a shadow</u> <u>of the things that were to come</u>; <u>the reality</u>, however, <u>is found in Christ</u>.

Colossians 2:14-17

"A shadow" means a foreshadow, testifying to the reality to come. But the real thing is not the shadow. Notice what verse 18 goes on to say:

Do not let anyone who delights in false humility and the worship of angels disqualify you. Such a person also goes into great detail about what they have seen; they are puffed up with idle notions by <u>their unspiritual mind</u>.

Colossians 2:18

Those who walk in the shadow of things to come rather than the reality of Christ have an "unspiritual mind," which means fleshly. This includes strict Sabbath-keepers. They're still trying to serve God from the perspective of the flesh no matter what staunch religious airs they put on. What irony!

The Physical Principle of the Sabbath

Although the Sabbath day law was a shadow that was fulfilled in Christ, the purely physical principle of the Sabbath — a day to cease from labor — remains true and applicable, but the believer has the freedom to pick that day or time slot. What I mean is that thousands of years before the Law was given to Israel, God set the example of working six days and resting one full day — completely taking a break from work, both mentally and naturally. This principle is healthy and is a wise principle by which to live. For example, I'm one of those people Paul spoke of who "considers every day alike" (Romans 14:5) and therefore I am not moved by national or religious holidays, which doesn't mean I won't celebrate them to some degree. But, whether I do or not, I'm free. It's the believer's choice according to his/her unique situation and schedule, as guided by the Holy Spirit.

In regards to the Sabbath — a day to cease from physical and mental toil — I celebrate Sabbaths once a week or as the need arises, as led of the Holy Spirit. For instance, just the other day I had finished a string of days of voluminous ministry work and I suddenly realized I was exhausted and needed a break. So I took a day off where I rested and didn't think of ministry toil — or any other type of work — at all. Once refreshed, I was inspired and psyched to finish the current project and tackle the next.

Are there examples of this in the New Testament? Yes. When Jesus sent out the twelve disciples to minister from village to village in Israel they drove out demons, cured diseases, preached the truths of God's kingdom and healed the sick. (Wouldn't it be awesome if more Christians ministered like this today?). When they returned and gave a good report of their activities they all "withdrew by themselves" to the town of Bethsaida (Luke 9:10). Why is this significant? Because Jesus recognized the need for ministers to retreat for rest and refreshing after significant ministry endeavors which naturally protects them from burnout. They enjoyed a Sabbath — a rest from their labors — regardless of what day it was.

This, of course applies to any type of work and not just ministry. It's the principle of the Sabbath — to rest from one's work and rejuvenate via the Fountain of Life (Psalm 36:9). And this doesn't have to be a full day either; you can (and should) have mini-Sabbaths every day. As Solomon said, there's "a time to weep and a time **to laugh**, a time to mourn and a time **to dance**" (Ecclesiastes 3:4). Even work can become an idol — and unhealthy — if it's done without moderation.

Who, When, Where and Why?

The strict Sabbath Law was meant **for a particular people, at a particular time, in a specific place** and **for an explicit purpose**. Let's consider all four of these…

Concerning the first two, we know the Sabbath Law was meant for the Israelites after their exodus from Egypt because the LORD didn't give the Sabbath to Adam, Eve, Cain, Noah, Abraham, Isaac, Jacob or Joseph & his brothers. In fact, after the mention of God resting when he completed the work of creating the heavens & the earth (Genesis 2:3), **there's zero mention of the Sabbath until the LORD gave Moses the Sabbath Law once the Israelites escaped slavery in Egypt**.

I want to stress that Abraham — our father of faith[7] — was not under the Sabbath day Law and did not observe it as a strict Law, although he no doubt took regular rests from his labor corresponding to the example of the Lord after creating the earth & universe. Resting like this is simply a matter of common sense. You don't need to be a spiritual Einstein to grasp that it's a healthy principle by which to live.

---

[7] See Romans 4:3,11.

The Sabbath day Law lasted until the new covenant was established:

> **By calling this covenant "new," <u>he has made the first one obsolete</u>; and what is obsolete and aging will soon disappear.**
>
> **Hebrews 8:13**

In our new and superior covenant we are instructed to not let anyone judge us in regards to a Sabbath day (Colossians 2:16-17). What does it mean to "not let anyone judge" you since it's impossible to prevent modern-day Pharisees from judging you and badmouthing you to others? Surely we should correct such people with the truth of Scripture, as the Spirit leads, but it more importantly refers to not allowing these legalists to cause *you* any distress. In other words, we are to have peace about the fact that the Sabbath Law is obsolete in our New Covenant regardless of what rigid legalists insist.

The Sabbath day Law was part of the Old Covenant and, as you can see above, that covenant became obsolete with the ushering in of the New Covenant. Christ plainly said that the Old Testament ended with John the Baptist (Luke 16:16) who prepared the way for the Messiah via a baptism of repentance (Luke 3:2-19). With the ministries of John and Jesus the kingdom of God was preached, not the Law and the Prophets. The four Gospels are not Old Testament, as some erroneously claim, but are rather the "prologue" to the New Testament and therefore *PART OF* the New Testament even though the Church didn't technically start until the Day of Pentecost (see Acts 11:15-16 & 2:1-13). This is why Christ spoke *AS IF* the Church was already in function in Matthew 18:17.

I emphasize this because strict Sabbath-keepers argue that the Sabbath day Law was a perpetual law based on what the LORD said to the Hebrews in this passage:

> " 'The Israelites are to observe the
> Sabbath, celebrating it for the generations to
> come as a <u>lasting</u> covenant. [17] It will be a sign
> between me and the Israelites <u>forever</u>' "
>
> **Exodus 31:16-17**

Two things: **1.** This passage is referring specifically to the
Israelites under the Old Covenant, which is **the context** of the
LORD's instruction and "Context is king," which is a
hermeneutical law. **2.** Another interpretational rule is that
"Scripture interprets Scripture" and other passages clearly show
that the Old Covenant is obsolete and that New Covenant believers
are not under the Mosaic Law. The ceremonial and dietary laws —
including the Sabbath day Law — foreshadowed Christ and are
therefore not applicable to New Covenant believers.

As far as the Israelites observance of the Sabbath Law
being a "lasting covenant" and "a sign between God and the
Israelites forever," this was true **as long as the Old Covenant was
in motion**. But it's not any longer. **It's obsolete!** We now have a
superior **covenant** (Hebrews 7:22 & 8:6,13)! Furthermore, the root
Hebrew word for "lasting" and "forever" in this passage is *olam
(oh-LAWM)*, which means "long duration" or "lasting," but not
necessarily never-ending in the absolute sense. I'll prove this
beyond any shadow of doubt momentarily.

Concerning the fact that the Sabbath Law was meant
specifically for people dwelling in the warm climate of Israel, this
can be observed in this additional element of the Law:

> **Moses assembled the whole Israelite
> community and said to them, "These are the
> things the Lord has commanded you to do: [2] For
> six days, work is to be done, but the seventh day
> shall be your holy day, a day of sabbath rest to
> the Lord. <u>Whoever does any work on it is to be</u>**

put to death. [3] **Do not light a fire in any of your dwellings on the Sabbath day.**"

Exodus 35:1-3

Verse three is understandable in light of the fact that lighting a fire would require considerable work, such as gathering kindling & wood and vigorously rubbing sticks together for the friction to spark a flame. But it doesn't say a person/family can't maintain a fire from the previous day, which means they would have to collect the necessary lumber in days prior, not to mention periodically feed the fire on the Sabbath.

But this particular detail would present problems for people living in colder climates, especially in the winter months. Having a fire in such regions can be a matter of life or death. If their fire went out — which is entirely conceivable — would they be prohibited from starting a new one at the risk of the penalty of death? This shows that this rigid law was intended for the Hebrews dwelling in the generally warm climate of Israel, not people living in Scandinavia, Siberia, Alaska, Labrador or Cape Horn.

As far as the purpose of the Sabbath Law — and, the Law (Torah) in general — we discovered in previous chapters that it was given so that transgression would increase and drive the Israelites' to the Savior, Jesus Christ (Romans 5:20). The New Testament puts it like this:

So **the law was put in charge to lead us to Christ** **that we might be justified by faith.** [25] **Now that faith has come, we are no longer under the supervision of the law.**

Galatians 3:24-25

This includes no longer being *under* the strict Sabbath day Law, although — as noted earlier — it's healthy to partake of the *principle* of the Sabbath by enjoying periodic rests from our work as led of the Spirit.

Something to Consider

The Sabbath Law was given to the Israelites thru Moses 3500 years ago and it was only to last until the establishment of the New Covenant, which means it was only relevant for roughly 1500 years. Here's a pertinent question: In the 3500 years since God gave this Law for those under the Old Covenant, don't you think it's highly possible that somewhere in those thousands of years that the seventh day of the week of the Hebraic calendar got off by a day or two or three? In other words, how do we know our current Saturday is the *real* seventh day according to the original Hebrew calendar? What if it's off by 2-3 days and Monday or Tuesday is the actual Sabbath day? Or Thursday or Friday?

A Sabbath-keeper would likely answer: "Well, God knows your heart; so even if you're practicing the Sabbath on the technically wrong day it's okay. And, besides, the LORD would adjust his judgment based on what the seventh day is within one's culture." This basically agrees with my earlier point about freely practicing the *principle* of the Sabbath — resting from one's labors — by faith as the Spirit directs: **In the new covenant we don't go by quaint obsolete ceremonial laws, but are to be led by the Spirit according to our unique situation and schedule.** Let me give an example:

For 9 years from 1986-1995 I had a schedule where I worked Saturday morning and Sunday night (as well as most of the week days). In other words, I worked every weekend 17 hours. The LORD blessed me with this job for that season in my life; it fit my lifestyle and I appreciated it. As such, I would rest on Monday or Tuesday. In short, I was observing the principle of the Sabbath as led of the Spirit according to the schedule with which God blessed me.

Answering Various Questions/Arguments on the Sabbath

Let's wrap-up this chapter by considering various questions or arguments concerning the Sabbath…

'Is Sunday the "Christian Sabbath"?'

No, the first day of the week — Sunday — was referred to by early Christians as "the Lord's day" (Revelation 1:10) and they gathered, ate and worshipped together on Sunday for two scriptural reasons:

1. Sunday was the day it was discovered that Christ's tomb was empty and he had risen from the dead (Matthew 28:1-7, Mark 16:1-16 & Luke 24:1-7). All three of these passages plainly state that these events occurred on "the first day of the week."
2. There are seven references in Scripture of the Lord appearing to the disciples before his ascension and five of these times God's Word indicates that Jesus met them on the first day of the week (e.g. John 20:19). The other two times the specific day is not noted. During these encounters Christ was honored and he taught from the Scriptures, ate with the disciples, breathed the Holy Spirit on them and commissioned them (see, for example, Luke 24:13-49 and John 20:19-29). These items sure sounds like a Christian service to me!

As far as extra-biblical testimony goes, Ignatius of Antioch (circa 35-107 AD) was a disciple of the apostle John and he referred to the "the Lord's day" as the day that Jesus rose from the dead: "If, therefore, those who were brought up in the ancient order of things have come to the possession of a new hope, **no longer observing the Sabbath**, but living in the observance of **the Lord's Day**, on which also our life has sprung up again by Him and by His death" (Magnesians 9:1).

'Didn't Roman Emperor Constantine the Great issue an edict in 321 AD making Sunday an official day of rest?'

Yes, he did, so what? What politicians did three centuries after Christ had no bearing on the scriptural facts or the beliefs/practices of the early believers, as detailed earlier.

For further proof, the 2nd century Christian apologist, Justin Martyr (100-165), said: "But **Sunday is the day on which we all hold our common assembly**, because it is the first day on which God, having wrought a change in the darkness and matter, made the world; and **Jesus Christ our Savior on the same day rose from the dead**." [8] This was over 150 years *before* Constantine issued his edict.

'Isn't meeting on Sunday pagan since the name "Sunday" stems from Hellenistic astrology?'

All seven of our days of the week were named after the planets of Hellenistic astrology, including Saturday, which was named after the Roman god Saturn. So, by this line of reasoning,

---

[8] *1 Apol. LXVII* in *Ante-Nicene Fathers: The Apostolic Fathers with Justin Martyr and Irenaeus, Vol. 1*, Ed. A. Cleveland Coxe (Grand Rapids, MI: Eerdmans, 2001), 186.

worshipping on any of these days is "pagan." Needless to say, this argument is silly.

'The Old Testament says that the Sabbath is a "lasting covenant" and is a sign between God and the Israelites "forever".'

This argument is based on what is said in Exodus 31:16-17. The root Hebrew word for "lasting" and "forever" in this passage is *olam (oh-LAWM)*, which means "long duration" or "lasting," but not necessarily never-ending in the absolute sense. So in the context of Exodus 31:16-17 (remember: "Context is king") it means **lasting as long as the Israelite's covenant was in operation**. This turned out to be about 1500 years, which is when Christ came.

In support of this conclusion, *olam* is also used in reference to circumcision, (Genesis 17:10-14), but we saw in the previous chapter that physical circumcision is not relevant in the New Covenant; it was only relevant to the Abrahamic Covenant and the Mosaic Covenant.

Olam is also used in reference to animal sacrifices (Leviticus 7:36-38) and yet the need to sacrifice animals ceased with the spilling of Christ's blood (Hebrews 9:23-10:12).

Similarly, the Levitical priesthood was said to be a "lasting" (*olam*) ordinance in Exodus 29:7-9, but the New Testament clearly shows that it ended with the Mighty Christ, a priest in the order of Melchizedek, not Aaron (Hebrews 7:11-12).

I could go on and on here, but I think you can see that the Hebrew word *olam* used in reference to Sabbath-observance meant "lasting" only as long as the Mosaic covenant was in operation.

As for the phrase in Exodus 31:16: "The Israelites are to observe the Sabbath, celebrating it **for the generations to come** as a lasting (*olam*) covenant," this simply means that Sabbath-observance was to be practiced for the many generations to come as long as their *olam* covenant was in effect. However, this long-lasting covenant is no longer in effect ever since Christ came.

'Observing the Sabbath appears to be practiced during eternity, so why would it be removed during the Church Age?'

This question is addressed in chapter **11**, along with a similar question about the Millennium.

8
—

Holy-Days and Holidays

Occasionally I come across believers — face to face or in writing — who rant & rave over holidays. They insist that certain holidays shouldn't be celebrated by genuine Christians while certain others should be observed. For instance, they'll decry the somewhat dubious origins of, say, Christmas and Easter and lambaste those who celebrate these holidays. Naturally, some insist that the Jewish festivals and the Sabbath must be strictly observed in order to please God.

A good example of how annoying this can be took place last St. Patrick's Day when my wife, Carol, had the audacity to wear a green jacket to work with a shamrock pin. An immature Christian coworker lambasted her for following a supposedly "pagan" holiday. Not being one to get into strife, particularly over minor issues, sweetie Carol informed the coworker that she was Irish. The woman responded, "Well, I'm German, should I celebrate Hitler?" (Rolling my eyes).

Irksome confrontations like this are unnecessary and irrelevant in light of what God's Word says on the topic of holidays. Since Christians are under the New Testament — the New Covenant, which means *new contract* with God — I encourage believers to embrace **what the New Testament teaches on holidays**. Notice what it says:

> **Accept the one whose faith is weak, without quarreling over disputable matters. [2] One person's faith allows them to eat anything, but another, whose faith is weak, eats only vegetables. [3] The one who eats everything must not treat with contempt the one who does not, and the one who does not eat everything must not judge the one who does, for God has accepted them. [4] Who are you to judge someone else's servant? To their own master, servants stand or fall. And they will stand, for the Lord is able to make them stand.**
> **[5] <u>One person considers one day more sacred than another; another considers every day alike. Each of them should be fully convinced in their own mind.</u> [6] <u>Whoever regards one day as special does so to the Lord</u>. Whoever eats meat does so to the Lord, for they give thanks to God; and whoever abstains does so to the Lord and gives thanks to God.**
>
> **Romans 14:1-6**

The apostle Paul brings up two "disputable matters" in this passage: In verse 2 he mentions the issue of eating everything or being a vegetarian; in verse 5 he remarks how some consider certain days holy — i.e. "holi-days" — while others consider every day the same. The person who has the fuller knowledge and understanding on the issue is "strong" while the person with lesser revelation is "weak" (see 15:1).

While the issue of holidays is not necessarily a matter of being "strong" or "weak" because it's often simply an issue of preference, a person's preference could be the result of fuller knowledge, which means that person is "strong." The person who acts out of lesser knowledge or ignorance, by contrast, is "weak."

Many believers celebrate Christmas and Easter because these days represent to them the birth and resurrection of Christ respectively. There are others, however, who don't celebrate them for one reason or another or, at least, are indifferent. It's a matter of preference or opinion, regardless of one's reasons. As Paul taught, "Each one should be fully convinced in his own mind."

"Accept One Another… in Order to Bring Praise to God"

Regardless, the one who has the fuller understanding is not to look down on the one with the lesser because it would be arrogant. Similarly, the one with the lesser revelation must not condemn the one with the fuller. You could insert any non-essential doctrine or issue into this scenario and it would apply.

Paul concluded the matter with these powerful words:

> **<u>Accept one another</u>, then, just as Christ accepted you, in order to bring praise to God.**
> **Romans 15:7**

Whether someone is "strong" with fuller revelation or "weak" with lesser, we are to accept one another just as Christ accepted us! Furthermore, doing this brings praise to God! Do you want to bring praise to God? Of course you do. Then be sure to warmly accept brothers and sisters in the Lord who disagree with you on non-essential matters, like wearing a green jacket and shamrock pin on St. Patrick's Day. ☺

Nowhere does the Bible say we are to get into eye-rolling arguments or cancel relationships due to non-essential doctrines or issues, like which holidays a believer observes or doesn't observe. On the contrary, we're **to accept one another**.

The only just reasons for breaking relations with other believers or so-called believers are:

1. If the person advocates false teaching on essential matters, like the Lordship of Christ or the importance of keeping in repentance;
2. If the individual refuses to repent of a legitimate transgression (Matthew 18:15-17); or...
3. If the person is incorrigibly contentious or fleshly (Romans 16:17-18 & 2 Timothy 3:1-5).

It's important to keep in mind, however, that in all these cases the offending individual should be prayed for and should receive the warm hand of fellowship if s/he makes a 180 at some point, like the fornicator who repented and was welcomed back into the Corinth church (2 Corinthians 2:6-11). The person should not be gossiped about and mocked. The Bible says to "slander no one" (Titus 3:2), even if s/he is guilty of a sin and has been dis-fellowshipped from the assembly.

In any event, when you see brothers or sisters in the Lord who are quick to argue or cease fellowship over non-essential issues, including holidays, you can be sure they're either spiritually immature or infected by rigid Sectarianism (a form of legalism[9]),

_____

[9] Sectarianism is **faction-ism**, which is actually cited as a work of the flesh in the Bible (Galatians 5:19-21). In the Greek it's *hairesis (HAH-ee-res-is)*, meaning "a religious or philosophical **sect**" and the resulting division it causes. As such, some translations render the word as "divisions." It's a "self-chosen opinion" rooted in sectarian loyalty — i.e. it's based on the beliefs of one's favored sect — rather than a viewpoint rooted in the rightly-divided Word of God. The Pharisees and Sadducees were strict sectarians and their faction-ism prevented them from seeing obvious truths in Scripture, even though they diligently

or both. It's sad because this needlessly separates Christians and, just as bad, limits the lives of those with lesser revelation.

What Is the "Fuller Knowledge" on Holidays?

Since the Bible says that the person who has the fuller knowledge and understanding on an issue is "strong" while the person with lesser revelation is "weak," you're probably wondering: What is the "fuller knowledge" on holidays for the New Testament believer? These verses plainly show us:

> [5] **One person considers one day more sacred than another; another considers every day alike. Each of them should be fully convinced in their own mind.** [6] **Whoever regards one day as special does so to the Lord.** Whoever eats meat does so to the Lord, for they give thanks to God; and whoever abstains does so to the Lord and gives thanks to God.
>
> **Romans 14:5-6**

This passage offers additional insight:

> **Therefore do not let anyone judge you by what you eat or drink, or with regard to a religious festival, a New Moon celebration or a Sabbath day.** [17] These are **a shadow** of the things

---

studied the Scriptures (John 5:39-40). Sectarian ministers are essentially "yes men" to their sect (party) whereas more independent ministers are naturally more reliable *if* they honestly focus on God's Word. This *does not* mean, of course, that if you belong to a sect — like Baptists — you're automatically guilty of sectarianism.

that were to come; <u>the reality</u>, however, <u>is found in Christ</u>.

Colossians 2:16-17

The Jewish festivals, the New Moon celebration and the Sabbath were mere **shadows** of what was to come — Jesus Christ! The kosher laws, feast days and holy-days that God commanded in the Mosaic Law — including the Sabbath — pictured the person and work of the coming Messiah. Jesus carried out all these types through his service on earth. Thus the need to observe them has ceased.

"A shadow" means a *foreshadow*, which directs us to the actuality to come. The real thing, of course, is not the shadow. Observe what verse 18 goes on to say:

Do not let anyone who delights in false humility and the worship of angels disqualify you. Such a person also goes into great detail about what they have seen; they are puffed up with idle notions by their <u>unspiritual mind</u>.

Colossians 2:18

Those who walk in the shadow of things to come rather than the reality of Christ have an "unspiritual mind," which means carnal. This includes strict Sabbath-observers and those who insist on observing the Judaic holy-days. They're still trying to serve God from the perspective of the flesh no matter what airs of religious devotion they put on.

Simply put, the Jewish festivals, the New Moon celebration and the Sabbath belong to the Old Covenant that Israel had with the LORD and have been done away. Let's consider a few relevant passages...

> **For when the priesthood is changed, <u>the law must be changed also</u>.**
>
> **Hebrews 7:12**

In our New Covenant Jesus Christ is our high priest (Hebrews 2:17 & 4:14). The priesthood has changed and thus the law has also changed. This includes ceremonial laws like the Jewish festivals, the New Moon celebration and the Sabbath, which have been done away:

> **⁵ They serve at a sanctuary that is a copy and shadow of what is in heaven. This is why Moses was warned when he was about to build the tabernacle: "See to it that you make everything according to the pattern shown you on the mountain." ⁶ <u>But in fact the ministry Jesus has received is as superior to theirs as the covenant of which he is mediator is superior to the old one</u>, since <u>the new covenant is established on better promises</u>...**
> **¹³ <u>By calling this covenant "new," he has made the first one obsolete</u>; and what is obsolete and outdated will soon disappear.**
>
> **Hebrews 8:5-6,13**

What about the moral law, how has it changed? Let me explain:

As plainly observed in this passage, the New Covenant that believers have with God is superior to the Old Covenant that the Israelites had. The New Covenant is superior because we've been released from the Law — the Torah — and serve in the new way of the Spirit wherein we receive spiritual regeneration (Ephesians 4:22-24), not in the Old Covenant way of the written code, i.e. the

Law. This is great because "the letter **kills**, but the Spirit **gives life**" (2 Corinthians 3:6).

Repentance and faith are **the conditions** for entering into the New Covenant (Acts 20:21 & Hebrews 6:1) and **the terms** are "faith working through love," which means faith is activated by love (Galatians 5:6 Amplified). When we walk out of love[10] we walk out of faith and thus our faith won't work, which isn't good because faith is the foundation of our covenant. Why is "faith working through love" so important? Because love is the fulfillment of the moral Law, as Christ points out here:

> [36] **"Teacher, which is the greatest commandment in the Law?"**
>
> [37] **Jesus replied: " 'Love the Lord your God with all your heart and with all your soul and with all your mind.'** [38] **This is the first and greatest commandment.** [39] **And the second is like it: 'Love your neighbor as yourself.'** [40] **All the Law and the Prophets hang on these two commandments."**
>
> **Matthew 22:36-40**

This has been stressed before, but it needs repeated: All the Old Testament moral laws can be compressed into two basic rules with three applications: LOVE GOD & LOVE PEOPLE as you LOVE YOURSELF. When you do this you realize all the moral Law. How so? Because the believer who loves God, loves others and loves himself/herself will cultivate a relationship with the LORD and learn to walk according to his/her new righteous nature with the help of the Holy Spirit, which automatically fulfills the moral Law (Romans 8:4).

---

[10] As defined in 1 Corinthians 13:4-7.

It's important to stress that loving others means walking in tough love *when necessary* just as much as it means walking in gentle love. There are numerous examples of Jesus and Church leaders walking in tough love when applicable (e.g. Matthew 23:13-35, Mark 11:15-18, Acts 8:17-24 & 13:8-12).

This "law of love" automatically fulfills all the moral law of the Old Testament and is one-in-the-same as the "law of Christ" (Galatians 6:2 & 1 Corinthians 9:21).

Closing Word on Holidays

Now you know what the New Testament teaches about holidays and I hope it sets you free (John 8:31-32). If you come across legalists who rant & rave that "Christians can celebrate this and that holiday but not this or that holiday" you can disregard their words as the result of lesser knowledge or ignorance; or perhaps the infection of legalism. But continue to accept them, pray for them, walk in love with them and correct them through God's Word when appropriate as led of the Spirit, which is a form of tough love.

Whilst some religious holidays have somewhat questionable origins, observing them or not is a matter that comes down to a person's current perception and preference thereof. For example, Christmas may be about materialism to one person — which isn't good — and it may be about a celebration of Christ and the gift of giving to another — which is good; Easter may be about hedonistic spring break to one person — which isn't good — and about the resurrection of Christ and spiritual regeneration to another — which is good. This is why Paul by the Holy Spirit encouraged Christians to resist making judgments about fellow believers and the days they choose to celebrate as holidays (Romans 14:5-8 & Colossians 2:16).

9
—

The Purpose of the Sabbath Rests

What was the purpose of the Sabbath day? I mean beyond the fact that it's healthy to rest from labor one day a week. In other words, why was the Sabbath so important, even to the point of executing a person under the Old Covenant if they violated it?

The Big Picture: Relationship with God

What we're going to do in this chapter is look at **the big picture**. You see, God is obsessed with humanity in a positive way. The Bible is all about the Creator's *relationship* with human beings. The first three chapters of Genesis detail the LORD's creation of the heavens & the earth and all living things thereof, including the only beings created in God's image and likeness, our progenitors Adam & Eve. Genesis 3 records their unfortunate fall and the resulting curse on creation.

The rest of the Bible chronicles the implementation of God's brilliant plan of redemption, ending with the last two chapters of Revelation, which describe the eternal age of the new heavens and new earth with this wonderful everlasting reality:

> **"Look! God's dwelling place is now among the people, and <u>he will dwell with them</u>. <u>They will be his people</u>, and <u>God himself will be with them and be their God</u>. '<u>He will wipe every tear from their eyes</u>. There will be no more death' or mourning or crying or pain, for the old order of things has passed away."**
>
> **Revelation 21:3-4**

These facts show that **having a relationship with people is of immense importance to our Creator**. And this explains the lengths God has taken to supply a Redeemer for fallen humanity and reconcile with those wise, humble souls who are willing. To drive home how important genuine relationship is to our Creator, consider what the Lord will say to the false prophets who masqueraded as ministers when they stand before Him to be judged: "I never *knew* you" (Matthew 7:23). This explains why they're described as "false": They never actually **knew** the Lord.

With this understanding, let's consider…

The Original Sabbath

We know that the celebration of the Sabbath day once-a-week was for the immediate purpose of **resting** & **refreshing** (Exodus 23:12).

This harkened back to the original Sabbath — the rest — that God enjoyed with Adam & Eve *before* their fall from grace and the corresponding curse on physical creation, which introduced wearisome labor:

¹⁷ To Adam he said, "Because you listened to your wife and ate fruit from the tree about which I commanded you, 'You must not eat from it,'

"Cursed is the ground because of you;
through painful toil you will eat food from it
all the days of your life.
¹⁸ It will produce thorns and thistles for you,
and you will eat the plants of the field.
¹⁹ By the sweat of your brow
you will eat your food...

Genesis 3:17-19a

This is part of the Genesis curse, which introduced the concept of toilsome labor: One has to work "by the sweat of his/her brow" in order to merely live. Humankind has been under this curse ever since. The Sabbath day law was given to Israel in order to give them a break from this curse once a week — a day in which they could relax and recharge. Yet it was *more* as the Sabbath day looked back to the time when humanity didn't have to toil to survive and when the first humans enjoyed intimate fellowship with their Creator. The good news is that it will be like this again, in the eternal age of the new heavens and new earth (2 Peter 3:13); and partially during the Millennium.

Now here's something interesting to chew on: The prohibitions against working on the Sabbath in the Mosaic Law were utterly irrelevant to Adam & Eve and the ongoing Sabbath they enjoyed with the LORD *before* their fall. For instance, the Israelites weren't allowed to buy & trade on the Sabbath (Nehemiah 10:31 & 13:15-17), but Adam & Eve didn't need to buy & trade because they ate freely of the fruit of the Garden of Eden (Genesis 2:16). Moreover, the Israelites weren't allowed to kindle a fire (Exodus 35:3-3), but Adam & Eve didn't need a fire because they were perfectly warm in their glorified naked state. Nor did they need to cook meat because they were vegetarians, not to mention they couldn't even kill animals since death didn't exist yet. Actually, fire didn't exist either until after the Genesis curse was effected because fire is an element of entropy, the "bondage to decay" (Romans 8:21).

Furthermore, the Israelites were to delight in the LORD on the Sabbath (Isaiah 58:13-14), but Adam & Eve didn't need a command to do this on any particular day because they enjoyed joyful communion with the LORD 24/7.

All of this points to this conclusion: The observance of the Sabbath day law by the Israelites was **to act out in a cursed, immoral world what the first humans practiced in an idyllic, pure world**. The LORD was basically saying: "Remember what it was like when there was peace between God and humanity, when the Creator and the created enjoyed sweet fellowship continuously and you weren't 'slaves to the grind.' "

Jesus Christ is Our Sabbath Rest

Yet the Sabbath day was just a shadow of the Reality, Jesus Christ. Through the Messiah we have acquired what had been missing since Adam's fall and more:

> **Not only is this so, but we also boast in God through our <u>Lord Jesus Christ, through whom we have now received reconciliation.</u>**
> **[12] Therefore, just as sin entered the world through one man, and death through sin, and in this way death came to all people, because all sinned**
>
> **Romans 5:11-12**

So the Sabbath reminded the Israelites of the way it used to be for God & humanity before the fall — which is the way it's *supposed* to be — and thus the Sabbath also looked forward to the reconciliation that would be made available through the One in whom the Sabbath pointed to, the Messiah:

> **Therefore do not let anyone judge you by what you eat or drink, or with regard to a <u>religious festival</u>, a <u>New Moon celebration</u> or a <u>Sabbath day</u>. [17] These are <u>a shadow</u> of the things that were to come; <u>the reality</u>, however, is found <u>in Christ</u>.**
>
> **Colossians 2:16-17**

All the Hebraic holidays — the Passover, First Fruits and New Moon — were Sabbaths because the Israelites *rested* from their labor and celebrated the LORD & the things of God. They were mere shadows of the reality, which is only found *in Christ*, meaning in covenant with God through Christ.

Say someone you love and honor is casting a shadow; wouldn't it be absurd to try to embrace the shadow when the real person is right there? That's basically what modern Torah-worshippers are doing, like people in the Hebrew Roots movement, the Seventh-Day Adventists and the Armstrongites. They cling to the Sabbath law and the Judaic festivals when these are mere shadows pointing to the superior covenant of Jesus Christ *and more* — eternity with the LORD in "the new heavens and new earth, the home of righteousness" (2 Peter 3:13):

> **<u>The law</u> is only <u>a shadow</u> of <u>the good things that are coming</u> — not the realities themselves.**
>
> **Hebrews 10:1a**

So the Sabbath was a type & shadow of:

1. **The rest** believers have with the Lord in the New Covenant while strangers on this earth.
2. **The rest** of eternity with the Lord in the new heavens and new earth, which will bring humanity full circle to the rest Adam & Eve enjoyed with the Creator during the original

Sabbath in the Garden of Eden before their fall and ouster (Genesis 3:22-24).

Concerning the first one, the writer of Hebrews brings up "the seventh day" — the Sabbath — and concludes "for anyone who enters God's rest also rests from their works, just as God did from his" (Hebrews 4:4,10). Keep in mind that he was addressing believers who were tempted to revert back to the Law due to persecution and hardship. He's imploring them to rest from trying to gain the LORD's favor through the works of the Old Covenant Law.

Notice *where* he says true rest with God can be found:

For we also have had <u>the good news</u> proclaimed to us, just as they did; but the message they heard was of no value to them, because they did not share <u>the faith</u> of those who obeyed. [3] Now <u>we who have believed enter that rest</u>

Hebrews 4:2-3a

This corresponds to something Christ said:

"Come to me, all you who are weary and burdened, and <u>I will give you rest</u>. [29] Take my yoke upon you and learn from me, for I am gentle and humble in heart, and <u>you will find rest for your souls</u>. [30] For my yoke is easy and my burden is light."

Matthew 11:28-30

The Messiah is our Sabbath rest. The Sabbath and all the Judaic Holy-days pointed to the rest that can only be found in the Lord Jesus Christ:

1. **The rest** we have *in* him during our sojourn on this earth.
2. And **the rest** we'll enjoy *with* him for eternity in the new heavens and new earth.

While all this is good, it means nothing if believers are unable to relate to it and apply it to their everyday lives. As such, the rest of this chapter is devoted to helping us do this.

God's Rest: Knowing the Lord and Resting from *your* Works

New Covenant believers are *in* Christ and therefore *in* God's rest. The two markings of walking in God's rest are **1.** resting from religious works performed to acquire salvation or God's favor and, more importantly, **2.** knowing the Lord, which means cultivating and maintaining a relationship. Notice how Paul expressed this:

> **What is more, I consider everything a loss because of the surpassing worth of <u>knowing Christ Jesus my Lord</u>, for whose sake I have lost all things. I consider them garbage, that I may gain Christ [9] and be found <u>in him</u>, <u>not having a righteousness of my own that comes from the law</u>, <u>but that which is through faith in Christ—</u> the righteousness that comes from God on the basis of faith. [10] <u>I want to know Christ</u>...**
> **Philippians 3:8-10a**

Nothing was more important to Paul than *knowing* the Lord and he links this to righteousness that comes through faith in Christ — i.e. the New Covenant — as opposed to having his own righteousness that comes through trying to obey the Mosaic Law.

He goes so far as to say that he considers *everything* a loss compared to knowing the Lord — everything is *garbage* by comparison. This doesn't mean that *all* other things are necessarily bad — many things are obviously good (spouse, children, home, work, fitness, friendships, etc.) — but they're worthless *compared to* knowing and walking with Christ.

The Messiah said his purpose was "to give eternal life to all those [the Father has] given him" (John 17:2). He then conveyed the primary quality of eternal life: "Now this is eternal life: **that they know you, the only true God, and Jesus Christ**, whom you have sent" (John 17:3). Obtaining immortality through repentance & faith is the chief purpose of Christianity (2 Timothy 1:10 & Acts 20:21). But Jesus here defines the primary *quality* of eternal life: **Knowing God**. And this explains why the gospel of Christ is called "the message of reconciliation" (2 Corinthians 5:18-20). 'Reconciliation' means to turn from enmity to friendship. You see, the Creator of the universe & all living things wants to be **your friend** (John 15:14-15).

But how do you walk with God as a friend?

Examples of Walking in God's Rest

I read an article by a Christian woman years ago who said she decided to spend quality time with the LORD every morning. Before everyone else in her house awoke she would grab a coffee and sit in the living room for about an hour and simply commune with her Creator. There was no serious Bible studying involved or by-rote prayer; the focus was on simple, honest communion. By turning off all the gizmos (TV, radio, computer, smart phone) and the distracting noise thereof, she was able to get in tune with the Spirit of God. Some days she felt more of a connection than others but, nevertheless, doing this *revolutionized* her spiritual walk.

The awesome news for every New Covenant believer is that you can have these types of conversations with God throughout the day, every day — when you wake up in bed, when you're in the shower, when you're driving, when you're walking down the hall, in the evening, when you're walking your yard, etc. And you don't have to use archaic lingo either, like "thee" and "thou." Use your common, everyday language. Paul referred to this as "praying without ceasing" (1 Thessalonians 5:17 KJV) and the "fellowship of the Holy Spirit" (2 Corinthians 13:14). We have to get away from the idea that we only encounter God when we go to church gatherings once or twice a week. This is an Old Testament mentality. Let me explain…

Although the Holy Spirit was active amongst the Israelites in Old Testament times, it was much different than the way it is with believers in the New Testament. The Holy Spirit's work in that earlier era was limited and selective because the Israelites were spiritually un-regenerated, although they did have a covenant with God and there were glimmerings of what the Spirit's function would be in the new covenant. David, for instance, was a type of the New Testament believer. Yet there was no spiritual rebirth, no indwelling and no baptism of the Spirit, at least not in the thorough scale we enjoy today.

Simply put, the Israelites were not temples of the Holy Spirit as we are in the new covenant because they weren't spiritually regenerated (Titus 3:5). The temple of God was a literal temple — a building — and before that, a tent tabernacle. Both the Tabernacle of Moses and the Temple of Solomon housed God's presence via the Ark of the Covenant (Exodus 25:22). These structures were literally God's house (although His presence was hidden in the Holy of Holies where the Ark was located, which the High Priest would only enter once a year). For the Israelites to encounter God they literally had to go to the Tabernacle or Temple, but — Praise God — this isn't the way it is in our New

Testament period because believers are literally the temples of God through spiritual rebirth (1 Corinthians 3:16)!

So attending church gatherings at a church facility is not the primary way to connect with God in the New Testament era, although it is a *way* due to the corporate anointing, which Jesus spoke of in Matthew 18:20, not to mention the anointing of fivefold ministry gifts, detailed in Ephesians 4:11-13. Experiencing this "corporate anointing," however, doesn't require going to a specific building. It can take place wherever believers meet — a park, a street corner, the mall, someone's house, a vehicle, the workplace, etc. Even better: Since every believer is the temple of God in our New Covenant we can encounter the LORD every day. If you're not doing it already, I encourage you to get in the habit of fellowshipping with the LORD on a continual basis, 24/7. It'll revolutionize your walk.

Communing with God in Solitary Places

Jesus said "when you pray, go into your room, close the door and pray to your Father, who is unseen. Then your Father, who sees what is done in secret, will reward you" (Matthew 6:6). Christ was simply talking about finding a solitary place for prayer sessions where you have the freedom to honestly commune. This is in contrast to religious hypocrites who love to pray in front of others, which really isn't communion with God, but rather putting on a show to impress people, which is fakeness, (Matthew 6:5). 'Hypocrite' literally means "actor." This isn't to say, by the way, that it's wrong to pray with other believers, as is depicted in the Bible (Acts 12:12), just that it's wrong for believers to pray in front of others *for the purpose of* impressing them and proving how supposedly godly they are.

When Jesus said to "go into your room, close the door and pray" he was simply talking about finding a solitary place where it's just you and the LORD. It's interesting that Jesus "as was his habit" often went to solitary places **in the wilderness** to pray, as shown in Mark 1:35, Matthew 14:23 and Luke 22:39-41. How come? Because there's something about nature that's conducive to encountering the Creator.

I think this is why men in particular are attracted to outdoor activities — like hunting, hiking, kayaking, fishing, etc. — because on some primal level they encounter God who is revealed in creation (Psalm 19:1-4, 97:6 & Romans 1:20).

Focus on Relationship and Works will follow

Walking in God's rest and focusing on relationship is superior to trying to attain God's salvation or favor through religious works because doing the latter simply doesn't work, as the Old Testament shows. Focusing on relationship is effective because **works always follow genuine relationship with the LORD and the corresponding faith**.

This brings to mind the story of Martha & her sister Mary when the Messiah visited their abode:

> **As Jesus and the disciples were on their way, he came to a village where a woman named Martha opened her home to him. [39] She had a sister called <u>Mary, who sat at the Lord's feet listening to what he said</u>. [40] But <u>Martha was distracted by all the preparations</u> that had to be made. She came to him and asked, "Lord, don't you care that my sister has left me to do <u>the work</u> by myself? <u>Tell her to help me!</u>"**
>
> **[41] "Martha, Martha," the Lord answered, "you are worried and upset about many things, [42] but <u>only one thing is needed</u>, Mary has chosen <u>what is better</u> and it will not be taken away from her."**
>
> **Luke 10:38-42**

Martha was so focused on the busy-ness of working for the Lord that she unintentionally forsook what was most important, **1.** spending time with him and **2.** "listening to what he said," a reference to listening to the leading of the Spirit or spending quality time with God's Word. Martha was so involved with the work of her service — i.e. her ministry — that she got mad at someone else who was free of such concerns and spending quality time with the Lord. So mad, in fact, that she started demanding things from the very One she was supposed to be serving! She *TOLD* the Lord, "Tell her to help me!" This is what legalism does to people; it corrupts them to the point that they end up having the very opposite attitude they should have.

Serving God is a wonderful thing, but don't be foolish like Martha and get your priorities out of whack. Think about it, the Living Lord was AT HER HOUSE — the amazing miracle-worker — and all she does is run around in a whirlwind of activity? Mary chose what was more important on this occasion. There's a time for work, of course, but relationship with your Creator comes first and work will naturally spring from that. In other words, our service for the Lord must spring from our love for the Lord. Otherwise it's just religious works or, worse, putting on a show.

When James said that faith by itself, if it is not accompanied by action, is dead (James 2:17,26) he was simply pointing out that genuine faith produces results because it's more than just mental assent. He certainly wasn't saying that works produce salvation because it's clearly established elsewhere in Scripture that we're saved by God's graciousness through faith "not by works so that no one can boast" (Ephesians 2:8-9). This famous passage is followed up by something that wholly agrees with what James wrote: "For we are God's workmanship, created in Christ Jesus to do good works" (Ephesians 2:10). Again, genuine faith produces the corresponding works, but this is different than saying that works produce salvation, which is human religion. Let's not get the cart before the horse!

This very book is a good example. I didn't write this book to acquire eternal salvation or gain God's favor. It sprang from my *relationship* with the Lord and my run-ins with misguided people who insist that Christians are *under* the Law of Moses, like those in the Hebrew Roots movement. So I wrote this book out of my love for God and love for others. Love produced this work, not legalism. This is a New Covenant principle and explains Paul's commendation of folks for their "labor prompted by love" (1 Thessalonians 1:3).

All of this explains why the New Testament emphasizes *knowing* God, *knowing* Christ and the *communion* of the Holy Spirit (Ephesians 1:17 & 1 Thessalonians 4:5).

As you walk with the Lord, focusing on **relationship**, you'll discern works that you'll be inspired to do — small and great — and then you'll carry them out, which produces satisfaction and joy (John 4:34). It could be buying a needy individual some new work boots or starting a ministry but, whatever the case, these works will spring from walking **in God's rest** and not *working* to acquire salvation or favor.

10

Giving and "Tithing"

The New Testament encourages believers to "grow in the grace of giving" just as we grow in faith, knowledge and love (2 Corinthians 8:7). When Paul requested an offering for needy Christians in Jerusalem he said this to the Corinthian believers:

> **Consider this: Whoever sows sparingly will also reap sparingly, and whoever sows generously will also reap generously. [7] <u>Each of you should give what you have decided in your heart to give</u>, <u>not reluctantly or under compulsion</u>, for <u>God loves a cheerful giver</u>. [8]And God is able to make all grace abound to you, so that in all things, at all times, having all that you need, you will abound in every good work.**
>
> **2 Corinthians 9:6-8**

The LORD only wants believers to give out of a giving heart that's happy to give. God doesn't want us to give reluctantly or under compulsion — which includes being coerced by ministers preaching

THE LAW and the Believer

condemnation, aka 'condo'.[11] There's no condo in Paul's request for funds for needy Christians, as chronicled in 2 Corinthians 8-9. He shares the need, encourages the believers to give, stresses that they'll be rewarded, and then adds that they should only give what they *decide* to *gladly* give. This is the only way they'll be blessed for their giving; otherwise they'd be giving from the flesh to earn salvation or the minister's favor or whatever, which is what legalists, Hindus, Muslims and other religionists do.

Another thing we can get from this passage is that Paul didn't view believers as pawns to fund ministry projects which Paul considered important, including altruistic ones. He respected and loved the believers where they were spiritually and permitted them to *make up their own minds* as led of the Spirit (or not led of the Spirit).

Generosity in Giving is a Matter of Wisdom

Generous giving is simply a matter of wisdom, as shown in the biblical book of wisdom:

> **[24] One person gives freely, yet gains even more;**
> **another withholds unduly, but comes to poverty.**
> **[25] A generous person will prosper;**
> **whoever refreshes others will be refreshed.**
> **Proverbs 11:24-25**

The book of Proverbs isn't the Mosaic Law; it's simply a collection of pithy common sense principles. And, as you can see, generosity in giving is wise and encouraged. Those who do so will "gain even more," "prosper" and "be refreshed" whereas those who "withhold unduly" won't. This is the **law of reciprocity**…

---

[11] A spirit of condemnation (condo) isn't appropriate for New Covenant ministers — or believers in general — because "there is now **no condemnation** for those who are *in* Christ Jesus" - Romans 8:1.

"Give and it will be given to You"

Jesus emphasized the **law of reciprocity**:

> [37]"Do not judge, and you will not be judged.
> Do not condemn, and you will not be condemned.
> Forgive, and you will be forgiven. [38] Give, and it will
> be given to you. A good measure, pressed down,
> shaken together and running over, will be poured
> into your lap. For with the measure you use, it will be
> measured to you."
>
> Luke 6:37-38

The law of reciprocity simply means that you get what you give; you reap what you sow. This law doesn't just work with money, but with whatever you give out. In verse 37 Christ lists judging, condemning and forgiving as examples. It's not rocket science: If you're merciful to others, people will be merciful to you; if you're kind and respectful to others, people will show kindness and respect toward you. It's a general rule, though, and not an absolute law. For instance, just because you don't judge and condemn others it doesn't mean your enemies won't *ever* judge and condemn you. Jesus, for example, was a thoroughly innocent man who simply spoke the truth and he was murdered for it.

Verse 38 is an encouragement to "grow in the grace of giving," as Paul later put it (noted above), with the promise that you'll receive in return accordingly. The statement "Give and it will be given to you" doesn't even specify money, although the principle certainly includes the giving of money.

Generously giving to others should be rooted in the law of love — loving God and loving others as you love yourself. This is the New Covenant "law" on giving.

'What about the Tithe?'

The "New Testament" is **the new covenant** — the new contract — that God has with believers through Christ. It was established in chapter **1** that believers are **not under the Mosaic Law**, as verified by several clear passages, including Galatians 5:18, Romans 6:14 and this one:

> **...we have been <u>released from the law</u> to <u>live in the new way of the Spirit</u> NOT in the old way of the written code.**
>
> **Romans 7:6**

Believers are "released from the law" and serve "in the new way of the Spirit." This includes being released from the Law's command to pay tithes — which literally meant 10% of the Israelites' crops and livestock — to support the Tabernacle and Temple (see Leviticus 27:30, Numbers 18:26, Deuteronomy 14:24 and 2 Chronicles 31:5). Actually, the Law required a few tithes:

- **The main tithe** was for the Levites and the priests thereof (Leviticus 27:30), which was a tenth of the produce "from the land" and not income, which means that carpenters, masons and fishermen didn't pay it. God instructed that the Levites didn't get any real estate and that the LORD himself would be their inheritance. Thus the tithe is given to the Levites as their salary for Temple work and teaching. **This is the tithe that is commonly understood.**

- **The "second tithe"** (according to the Mishnah) was for the use at the Temple during the feasts (Deuteronomy 12:17 & 14:22-27), which was 10% of the remaining 90% **for personal consumption** at the festivals during 1st, 2nd, 4th and 5th annual cycles of the shmita (7-year sabbatical cycle). This is the festival tithe. Basically, Israelites would take a tenth and bring it to the Temple and **consume it there themselves**. You could call it a vacation fund. As such, it wasn't exactly a sacrificial gift to God because this portion would be spent on themselves for the celebration; their gift would simply be their obedience. It goes without saying that this second tithe shouldn't be calculated into the tithe totality.

- **The third tithe** was for the needy in the land on the third and sixth years (Deuteronomy 14:28-29 & 26:12). Every third year, instead of bringing the tithe to Jerusalem, it was to be stored up in the Israelites' hometowns for the poor. Mishnah says that this is the same 10% that is normally used for festivals, but every 3 years is diverted to the needy instead. In addition, produce from the edges of crops and gleanings were left for the poor (Leviticus 23:22). This was basically an ancient version of our Social Security or welfare system.

Together these amounted to roughly 12-13% of the Hebrews' agricultural and ranching produce, if you do the math.

So **the Old Testament tithe** was essentially a method of taxation in the Israel theocracy and, later, monarchy to provide for the needs of the priests & Levites in the religious system. **The second tithe** was used for personal consumption in celebration at the appropriate festivals while **the third tithe** supplied for the needy in the land.

Because the main tithe was 10% of produce "from the land," carpenters, masons and fisherman were exempt, which means that **Jesus didn't pay it**. However, he paid the Temple tax (Matthew 17:24-27) and — being God in the flesh — he was no doubt very generous with freewill offerings, which were completely voluntary contributions (Leviticus 23:38), as well as the giving of alms. He surely practiced the principle of firstfruits, which we'll get to momentarily.

New Covenant Giving

As noted earlier, the principle in the New Testament — *principle*, not Law — is to *willingly* and *cheerfully* give to support:

1. The needs of others (Acts 2:45 & Romans 15:25-27), which includes...
2. Supporting Christian workers — particularly those who teach and preach (more on this momentarily) — and...
3. Spreading the gospel through missionary outreach (Philippians 4:15-19). No amount is specified or commanded, nor is any percentage.

Some suggest that a tenth of one's earnings is a good standard (or starting point) for Christian giving based on the fact that Abraham — our "father of faith" — gave 10% of his earnings to the priest of Salem, who was a type of Christ, *before* the Mosaic Law was given and the corresponding command to pay tithes (which, again, literally means 10%). You can read about this in Hebrews 7:1-2.

Believers who rant & rave against tithing in the sense of the Old Testament Law are right since believers are clearly not *under* the Law, but it's significant that the New Testament cites this occasion where our father of faith gave 10% — a tithe — of his income to support a priest who was a type of Christ. Also consider this: If Abraham gave 10% of his earnings *before* the Law was introduced and the Law itself mandated the giving of 10%, shouldn't believers give at least 10% by the Spirit? Or perhaps I should put it like this: *Wouldn't* genuine believers give at least 10% of their income by the Spirit?

Speaking of those who rant & rave against tithing, one of their arguments is that pastors who teach on tithing are trying to put believers under the Law and therefore their ministries are cursed even as Paul cursed the Judaizers who were trying to get the Galatians under the Law (Galatians 1:6-9). But I know genuine pastors who preach tithing, **but they don't mean it in the sense of being under the Mosaic Law**, not at all. How do I know? Because I am familiar with them and their teachings. They're thoroughly New Testament-oriented — grace-oriented — not Law-oriented. As such, they mean "tithing" simply in the sense of giving 10% of one's income to support the assembly and all the financial needs thereof, which is in harmony with the fact that "tithe" simply means 10%.

This is not to say, however, that there aren't assemblies that are Law-oriented when it comes to giving. These are legalistic ministries that try to put people under the Law and are in essence preaching a "different gospel," as Paul put it in Galatians 1:6-9. If you observe this "**leave them**," as Christ instructed in Matthew 15:14.

In any case, **the early Church didn't appear to focus on a particular amount but rather on meeting needs as led of the Spirit, which sometimes meant giving much more than a tenth**. We observe this in that some believers sold homes or land to meet the needs that existed in the Christian community (Acts 4:34-37). This corresponds to

the aforementioned Galatians 5:18, which says that believers are led of
the Spirit and are not under the Law.

The Principle of the Firstfruits

The Bible supports the idea of offering the firstfruits of your
income to the LORD and his work. We see this in the book of wisdom,
which shows that those who honor God in this way will receive a
financial blessing:

> [11] **Honor the LORD with your <u>wealth</u>,**
>   **with the <u>firstfruits of all your crops</u>;**
> [10] **then your barns will be filled to overflowing,**
>   **and your vats will brim over with new wine.**
>   **Proverbs 3:9-10**

Is this a specific reference to obedience to Old Testament Law
— the Torah — or is it simply a principle of wisdom that more broadly
applies to all people who know God? It would seem the latter since, as
noted above, our father of faith, Abraham, gave a tenth of his income to
Melchizedek hundreds of years before the Law was given (Romans 4:11
& Hebrews 7:1-2). Again, Melchizedek was a type of Christ. Besides, as
noted earlier, the book of Proverbs isn't the Mosaic Law, but rather a
collection of wise principles on a myriad of practical issues.

In any case, a good example of the principle of the firstfruits can
be observed in Joshua's taking of Jericho where the Israelites didn't
plunder the city, but rather devoted it to the LORD (Joshua 6:21). This is
significant because pillaging a city was a means of resupplying armies
with food and equipment and **Jericho was the first city that the
Hebrews conquered in the Promised Land**. In other words, they
honored the LORD by giving the first victory to Him and sacrificing the
valuables thereof. The second city they took was Ai where they carried
off the plunder and livestock **for themselves** (Joshua 8:2).

While Christians are not under the Law, but rather are led of the
Spirit of God, the *principle* of the firstfruits applies. Old Testament
stories, like Abraham giving an offering to Melchizedek and Joshua

honoring the LORD with the valuables of Jericho, serve as *examples* or *illustrations* **to us**, as shown in 1 Corinthians 9:10, 10:6,11 and Galatians 4:24.

Your income may not even be cash but, whatever it is, honor God with your firstfruits, as led of the Holy Spirit. What work of the LORD should you give your firstfruits to? Obviously one that serves well and is impacting the world with the life-changing truths of the Word and the power of the Spirit. Don't give it to just any ol' impotent ministry.

I encourage giving proportionately to the work of the Lord using the tithe as **a pattern**. Although we are not cited percentages in the New Testament beyond Abraham's example with the priest of Salem, **the principle of proportionate giving** is illustrated (1 Corinthians 16:2 & 2 Corinthians 8). The New Testament also shows believers in the Church collecting to give to other ministries. Speaking of which…

Supporting Diligent Ministers Who Teach & Preach God's Word

As far as "supporting Christian workers — particularly those who teach and preach" goes, the New Testament instructs us to support those who diligently serve via the teaching & preaching of God's Word. Here are some obvious examples:

> **Let the one who is taught the word <u>share all good things with the one who teaches</u>.**
> **Galatians 6:6** (English Standard Version)

> **Who serves as a soldier at his own expense? Who plants a vineyard and does not eat its grapes? Who tends a flock and does not drink the milk? [8] Do I say this merely on human authority? Doesn't the Law say the same thing? [9] For it is written in the Law of Moses: "Do not muzzle an ox while it is treading out the grain." Is it about oxen that God is concerned? [10] Surely he says this for us, doesn't he?**

> Yes, **this was written for us**, because whoever plows and threshes should be able to do so in the hope of sharing in the harvest. [11] **If we have sown spiritual seed among you, is it too much if we reap a material harvest from you?** [12] If others have this right of support from you, shouldn't we have it all the more?
>
> But we did not use this right. On the contrary, we put up with anything rather than hinder the gospel of Christ. [13] Don't you know that those who serve in the temple get their food from the temple, and that those who serve at the altar share in what is offered on the altar? [14] In the same way, **the Lord has commanded that those who preach the gospel should receive their living from the gospel.**
>
> 1 Corinthians 9:7-14

> **The elders who rule well are to be considered worthy of double honor, especially those who work hard at preaching and teaching.** [18] For the Scripture says, "YOU SHALL NOT MUZZLE THE OX WHILE HE IS THRESHING," and "**The laborer is worthy of his wages.**"
>
> 1 Timothy 5:17-18

Verse 17 of the last passage says that those who "rule well" — referring to fivefold **leaders** (see Ephesians 4:11-13) — are worthy of receiving **double the honor**, specifically those who preach and teach God's Word. The Greek word for 'honor' means "a price; honor." So it's partially a *financial* term. A good example is Acts 7:16 where it refers to "the sum" of money Abraham used to purchase a tomb. The Greek for "double" means two-fold or, figuratively, an ample amount. With this understanding, fivefold ministers who labor diligently at teaching and preaching God's Word are "worthy of receiving double the honor." How much does an average laborer in your area make? Diligent ministers of the Word of God who are called and anointed to change the very trajectory of people's lives for the positive are worthy of double that amount.

Of course, genuine ministers are not to be "lovers of money," as shown in many passages, like 2 Timothy 3:2 and Luke 16:14. So, if you see a so-called minister who's obsessed with vapid materialism — i.e. conspicuous consumption — head for the hills. Christ said: "**Watch out! Be on your guard against all kinds of greed; a man's life does not consist in the abundance of his possessions**" (Luke 12:15).

However, this does not take away from the fact that ministers of the Word are to be financially supported by the people to whom they minister. By "ministers of the Word" I don't mean just pastors, but teachers, apostles, prophets and evangelists as well (Ephesians 4:11-13).[12]

If you're a believer and you're feeding heavily from a minister or ministry I encourage you to "grow in the grace of giving" and "share all good things with your instructor" (Galatians 6:6). Give only what you can cheerfully give as led of the Holy Spirit and you'll be blessed. Those who read the three passages above (amongst others) and continuously ignore them or try to write them off because of a spirit of freeloading stinginess are walking in disobedience and will be held accountable. See 2 Corinthians 5:10-11.

Allow me to give a personal example of supporting a ministry other than your local fellowship (although this applies to giving to your usual assembly as well). There's an international prophetic ministry that's been a blessing to Carol & me over the years and we've sown generously into it many times. Lately, however, money's been tight for various reasons and we haven't been supporting this ministry, but it's continued to bless us greatly on a regular basis. So I shared with Carol: "The next time a good donation comes in we need to sow 10% into this ministry." When a generous donation recently arrived we sowed roughly 12% into this inspirational ministry. Did we do this because we were under the Mosaic Law? Absolutely not. We did it because we were *led* of the Spirit. We did it because we *decided* to do it. We did it because we *wanted* to do it. And we did it *cheerfully*, not reluctantly.

---

[12] Pastors are important, but they're over-emphasized in the modern body of Christ at the expense of the other four giftings or anointings. Do a word study on the Greek terms for pastor and its synonyms (e.g. overseer, shepherd) and how often they're used in the New Testament in reference to Church leaders.

'What about "Your Tithe Belongs to the Local Church"?'

Pastors often use this phrase, but it can't be found in the New Testament. For one thing, New Covenant believers aren't under the Law and therefore aren't obligated to tithe, as already detailed. We're simply encouraged to "grow in the grace of giving" by supporting teachers & preachers who feed us, as well as helping needy Christians and supporting missionary outreaches. The amount of the offering we give to any of these can only be determined by the individual as led of the Spirit. It's a sum that each person decides upon and can give happily (and may not even be cash). If you're hooked up with a local ministry, seek the LORD about how much you should give to support it. Ten percent of your income is a good standard, as noted above.

But please don't forget about the many other ministries that reach people in ways that a local assembly cannot or does not. Is there a ministry, other than your local fellowship, that you feed from and has greatly blessed your walk with the Lord? Then, by all mean, "share all good things" with this ministry. Perhaps even consider "partnering" with it in support on a regular basis (Philippians 4:15 & 1:5).

Conclusion and *Suggestions* on Giving

Our conclusion from all this data is that the New Covenant believer is not under the Mosaic Law and therefore is not required to pay tithes in an Old Testament sense. In our superior covenant we are simply encouraged to live by the law of reciprocity and grow in the grace of giving.

However, giving 10% of your income to the work of God is a good starting place due to the pattern and **example** of Old Testament saints, like Abraham who gave 10% to Melchizedek, a type of Christ; not to mention the principle of firstfruits. If you can't give 10% cheerfully then I suggest starting with 7% or 5% or 2.5%. Seek the LORD in prayer and give joyfully as the Spirit directs.

Who should these monetary gifts go to? The ministries in which you feed off the most and enjoy the services thereof. If you enjoy the services of a particular ministry then — obviously — you should support it. You don't have to be a spiritual Einstein to grasp this.

With this understanding, you could give the whole shebang — the amount that you cheerfully decide to give — to your usual assembly. But if you feed off of other ministries you should naturally give a percentage to them. For instance, if you decide to go with (or start with) 10%, you could give 7% to your regular fellowship and 3% to other ministries.

You probably noted above that the Israelites gave about 3% of their roughly 13% of crop/ranch offerings to the poor. Using this as an example, not a rigid law, you can consider giving 3% of your income to the poor, which is above the 10% or whatever the amount is that you have decided to give.

You can offer this 3% to charities or leave room for the needs of others as they present themselves. For instance, when Paul requested an offering from the Corinthian believers for needy Christians in Jerusalem, they prayerfully searched their hearts and gave as they were willing & able.

A minister once told me that he "tithed 20%." This is an inaccurate statement because 'tithe' literally means "ten percent." What he meant to say was that he gave a double tithe; or that he tithed his income *plus* gave another tithe. I bring this up because it shows that this man had a plan for his giving, obviously based on directions from the Lord. In other words, he decided to give 20% because the Spirit led him to do so; and he was joyfully willing.

I encourage you to come up with **a plan** for giving in each season of your life based on God's leading. Even if you don't have any conventional income, you can give *something* according to your time & talents. A woman once gave me some pudding after I gave a sermon because she found out I loved butterscotch pudding.

These are just *suggestions* for you to consider as you focus on relationship with the LORD and "grow in the grace of giving."

Whatever you do, only give happily as led of the Spirit and you'll be blessed. Amen.

11

Addressing Various Objections

So the New Testament is clear that believers in Christ are not under the Mosaic Law, but rather fulfill the moral law by walking in the spirit. The only law we're under is the law of Christ, which is the law of love. The ritualistic and kosher laws are irrelevant in the New Covenant.

Despite the clarity and magnitude of the scriptural evidence on this issue, legalists who want believers under one element of the Law or another try to come up with loopholes to convince themselves and their potential converts. In this chapter we will examine their sixteen most popular objections...

'Jesus said that neither the smallest letter nor the least stroke of the pen would disappear from the Law *until* heaven & earth passed away and, since they haven't passed away yet, the Law hasn't either.'

This sounds like a legitimate argument until you closely read the passage and realize that it omits a pivotal statement Christ made. Here's the text:

> **¹⁷ "Do not think that I have come to abolish the Law or the Prophets; <u>I have not come to abolish them</u> but to fulfill them. ¹⁸ For truly I tell you, until heaven and earth disappear, not the smallest letter, not the least stroke of a pen, will by any means disappear from the Law <u>until everything is accomplished</u>."**
>
> **Matthew 5:17-18**

People who make the above argument usually leave out the last part. Christ plainly states that he didn't come to abolish the Mosaic Law in verse 17, but to fulfill it. This was the Messiah's purpose — to fulfill the Law. He goes on to say that neither jot nor tittle would "disappear from the Law **until** everything is accomplished."

So Jesus was not saying that the Law *wouldn't* pass away, but rather that **1.** He planned on fulfilling the Law & the Prophets, jots and tittles and all (which is what "the smallest letter" and "the least stroke of a pen" refer to) and **2.** the Law would become obsolete once he fulfilled it (Ephesians 2:15).

This crucial "until" is also noted in this passage:

> **Why, then, was the law given at all? It was added because of transgressions <u>until</u> the Seed [Christ] to whom the promise referred had come.**
>
> **Galatians 3:19a**

The Law was added **until Christ came and fulfilled it**. In other words, **the Law had an expiration date**…

> For God has done what the law, weakened by the
> flesh, could not do. By sending his own Son in
> the likeness of sinful flesh and for sin, he
> condemned sin in the flesh, [4] in order that <u>the</u>
> <u>righteous requirement of the law might be</u>
> <u>fulfilled in us,</u> <u>who walk not according to the</u>
> <u>flesh but according to the Spirit.</u>
>
> **Romans 8:3-4** (ESV)

When Jesus said that he had come to fulfill the Law and the
Prophets in Matthew 5, he had already **fulfilled** some notable
aspects, like the virgin birth (Matthew 1:22-23) and being called
out of Egypt (Matthew 2:13-15), as well as the reason why he was
called a Nazarene (Matthew 2:23). Torah-worshippers might argue
that, while Jesus was well on his way to fulfilling the Law and the
Prophets, he hadn't yet fulfilled *all* things. So when did Christ
technically fulfill *all* the Law and the Prophets? Here's when:

> Later, knowing that everything had now
> been finished, and so that <u>Scripture would be</u>
> <u>fulfilled</u>, Jesus said, "I am thirsty." [29] A jar of
> wine vinegar was there, so they soaked a sponge
> in it, put the sponge on a stalk of the hyssop
> plant, and lifted it to Jesus' lips. [30] When he had
> received the drink, Jesus said, "<u>It is finished.</u>"
> With that, he bowed his head and gave up his
> spirit.
>
> **John 19:28-30**

'Peter said that Paul's teachings were misunderstood'

Yes, Peter pointed out that some things Paul taught were
hard to understand and some people misinterpreted them. But does

this mean we can't take Paul's words to mean what they obviously say?

Let's start with what Peter actually said:

His letters contain some things that are hard to understand, which ignorant and unstable people distort, as they do the other Scriptures, to their own destruction.

2 Peter 3:16

All Peter says is that **some** of the Scriptures that the Holy Spirit moved Paul to write are hard to understand, which ignorant and unstable people distort **like they do other Scriptures**. So it's not just the Scriptures written through Paul that are misinterpreted by ignorant, unstable people.

Moreover, Peter doesn't specify which Scriptures are hard to understand and nowhere does the context suggest that Peter was referring to Paul's teachings about believers *not* being under the Law or that the ceremonial & dietary laws have ceased.

Furthermore, Peter himself testified that the Lord told him in a vision "Do not call anything impure that God has made clean," referring literally to unclean animals and figuratively to Gentile people (Acts 11:4-10). So by suggesting that ignorant people misinterpreted some portions of Scripture, Peter obviously wasn't saying that he disagreed with Paul's plain teachings on all foods being declared clean for believers.

Paul was a former Pharisee who followed the Torah to a 'T' and is second only to Jesus Christ as far as New Testament personages go. With this in mind, I think it's notable to point out that the LORD used Paul to write more of the New Testament than any other person, about one-third (not including Hebrews, which many believe he wrote); and half of the book of Acts is devoted to his missionary exploits.

With this in mind, what did this ex-Pharisee who formerly followed the Mosaic Law to a 'T' plainly teach about believers and what they could and couldn't eat & drink? Let's read:

> **I am convinced, being <u>fully persuaded in the Lord Jesus,</u> <u>that nothing is unclean in itself</u>. But if anyone regards something as unclean, then for that person it is unclean. [15] If your brother or sister is distressed because of what you eat, you are no longer acting in love. Do not by your eating destroy someone for whom Christ died.**
>
> **Romans 14:14-15**

> **For <u>the kingdom of God is not a matter of eating and drinking</u>, but of righteousness, peace and joy in the Holy Spirit.**
>
> **Romans 14:17**

> **Do not destroy the work of God for the sake of food. <u>All food is clean</u>, but it is wrong for a person to eat anything that causes someone else to stumble.**
>
> **Romans 14:20**

> **But <u>food does not bring us near to God</u>; we are no worse if we do not eat, and no better if we do.**
>
> **1 Corinthians 8:8**

> **Therefore do not let anyone judge you by what you eat or drink**
>
> **Colossians 2:16**

> **The Spirit clearly says that in later times some will abandon the faith and follow deceiving**

spirits and things taught by demons. ² Such teachings come through hypocritical liars, whose consciences have been seared as with a hot iron. ³ They forbid people to marry <u>and order them to abstain from certain foods,</u> <u>which God created to be received with thanksgiving</u> <u>by those who believe and who know the truth.</u> ⁴ For <u>everything God created is good, and nothing is to be rejected if it is received with thanksgiving,</u> ⁵ because it is consecrated by the word of God and prayer.

1 Timothy 4:1-5

Are these passages hard to understand or are they plain-as-day? Paul says, "For everything God created is good, and nothing is to be rejected if it is received with thanksgiving" (1 Timothy 4:4). Is there anything hard to understand about this statement? What Paul says in these passages corresponds to what Jesus taught on the topic:

"Are you so dull? Don't you see that <u>nothing that enters a person from the outside can defile them</u>? ¹⁹ For it doesn't go into their heart but into their stomach, and then out of the body." (<u>In saying this, Jesus declared all foods clean</u>.)

Mark 7:18-19

First Timothy 4:3 (cited above) plainly says that false teachers will rise up during the Church Age and teach things taught by deceiving spirits, including ordering believers "to abstain from certain foods, which God created to be received with thanksgiving by those who believe." Have you run into some believers or a sect that do this? **They're following deceiving spirits; get away from them!** See Christ's instructions in Matthew 15:14 for support. Of course, if you show them the New Covenant facts and they change their minds, there's no need to separate from them.

One last thing about 2 Peter 3:16, Peter says that "ignorant and unstable people distort" Paul's teachings "as they do the other Scriptures." I'd like to humbly point out that I don't qualify for this description as I'm hardly ignorant of the Scriptures since this ministry — Fountain of Life — focuses on teaching from God's Word in a sound and balanced manner with no concern to sectarian bias. We follow Paul's Spirit-led instruction to the churches: "**Do not go beyond what is written**" (1 Corinthians 4:6). As far as instability goes, I've been in the Lord since I was 20 years-old — 1984 — and I've never backslid in the conventional sense (i.e. I never went back into the world and acted like God didn't exist, etc.). I'm not saying that I know it all or that I'm not open to correction, because both are untrue; I'm just pointing out that I don't fit Peter's criteria of ignorant, unstable people whom "distort" the Scriptures.

'Matthew's version of Mark 7:19 *explains* that Jesus was talking about eating with unwashed hands'

Let's read the full passage from Mark:

> **Again Jesus called the crowd to him and said, "Listen to me, everyone, and understand this. [15] <u>Nothing outside a person can defile them by going into them</u>. Rather, it is what comes out of a person that defiles them."**
>
> **[17] After he had left the crowd and entered the house, his disciples asked him about this parable. [18] "Are you so dull?" he asked. "Don't you see that <u>nothing that enters a person from the outside can defile them</u>? [19] For it doesn't go**

into their heart but <u>into their stomach, and then</u> <u>out of the body.</u>" (<u>In saying this, Jesus declared</u> <u>all foods clean.</u>)

[20] He went on: "What comes out of a person is what defiles them. [21] For it is from within, out of a person's heart, that evil thoughts come—sexual immorality, theft, murder, [22] adultery, greed, malice, deceit, lewdness, envy, slander, arrogance and folly. [23] All these evils come from inside and defile a person."

Mark 7:14-23

What the Lord is saying is so clear that I hardly need to comment: In verses 18-19 he says that nothing that enters a person's body from the outside — i.e. food — can defile them because it doesn't go into the heart (the core of the mind) but rather into the stomach and then out of the body. Mark adds a parenthetical statement by the Spirit explaining that, "In saying this, Jesus declared all foods clean." This is a simple-to-understand explanation of what Christ was saying. There's no vagueness whatsoever. In the remaining verses the Messiah goes on to point out that evil originates from within and this is what defiles a person, not food.

Now let's look at Matthew's account of the same event or perhaps it's a similar event:

Then the disciples came to him and asked, "Do you know that the Pharisees were offended when they heard this?"

[13]He replied, "Every plant that my heavenly Father has not planted will be pulled up by the roots. [14] Leave them; they are blind guides. If the blind lead the blind, both will fall into a pit."

¹⁵ Peter said, "Explain the parable to us."

¹⁶ "Are you still so dull?" Jesus asked them. ¹⁷ "Don't you see that whatever enters the mouth goes into the stomach and then out of the body? ¹⁸ But the things that come out of a person's mouth come from the heart, and these defile them. ¹⁹ For out of the heart come evil thoughts—murder, adultery, sexual immorality, theft, false testimony, slander. ²⁰ These are what defile a person; but eating with unwashed hands does not defile them."

Matthew 15:12-20

As you can see, Matthew's account omits Mark's Spirit-led parenthetical explanation — "In saying this, Jesus declared all foods clean" — and it doesn't expound upon it either. As for Jesus' statement in verse 20, "These are what defile a person; but eating with unwashed hands does not defile them", this has nothing to do with whether or not Christ declared all foods clean, but rather addresses the Pharisees original question from verse 2: "Why do your disciples break the tradition of the elders? They don't wash their hands before they eat!"

Enough said.

'In Mark 7 Jesus did not teach that every animal is now clean and good for eating by actually doing so. If he did, the Pharisees and Israelites would have had a solid reason for doubting that He was the Messiah'

The relevant verses from Mark 7 are quoted in the previous section above where the end of verse 19 declares "In saying this, Jesus declared all foods clean." This is an explanatory statement given to Mark by the Spirit. It reveals the obvious implications of what Jesus said and points to the freedom from the dietary laws for new covenant believers.

In his actual life on earth, however, Jesus fulfilled the Law, including the dietary laws, which is precisely what he said he came to do (Matthew 5:17). As such, legalists like the Pharisees and Teachers of the Law couldn't nail him for being disobedient to any part of the Law, whether moral, ritualistic, dietary or civil. Christ had to do this in order to be a perfect substitutionary sacrifice which paved the way for our superior New Covenant with God.

In this new covenant, all foods are declared clean and this is precisely what the passage says. If the plain sense makes sense — and is in harmony with the rest of the New Testament — don't look for any other sense lest you end up with nonsense.

'How were all foods declared clean when the book of Revelation refers to certain birds as unclean at the end of the Tribulation'

Let's read the passage in question:

> **After this I saw another angel coming down from heaven. He had great authority, and the earth was illuminated by his splendor. ² With a mighty voice he shouted:**
>
> **" 'Fallen! Fallen is Babylon the Great!'**
> **She has become a dwelling for <u>demons</u>**
> **and a haunt for every <u>impure spirit</u>,**
> **a haunt for every <u>unclean and detestable bird</u>."**
>
> Revelation 18:1-2

Since "every unclean and detestable bird" is used in direct connection with demons and impure spirits in the previous two lines it's obviously a figurative reference to these. Another example of this can be observed when Jesus said, "I have given you authority to trample on snakes and scorpions and to overcome all the power of the enemy" (Luke 10:19); Christ obviously wasn't referring to literal snakes and scorpions but to the devil and demonic spirits.

This is supported by the fact that the bulk of verse 2 is in poetic mode in the form of synonymous parallelism wherein the latter part of the verse repeats the first part in different words.

But's let's say Revelation 18:2 *is* referring to literal unclean birds. These birds are unclean according to Old Testament dietary laws, so what? The text doesn't say anything whatsoever about whether or not believers are obligated to obey such dietary laws. To properly understand that topic we must go to the passages that directly address *that* topic, like the ones cited above. This is in line with the hermeneutical rule that Scripture interprets Scripture where the more direct and detailed passages naturally trump the indirect and ambiguous ones. Since Revelation 18:1-2 says nothing about whether or not believers have the freedom to eat foods considered unclean for the Israelites under the Old Covenant we simply go to the passages that directly and clearly address that issue.

Furthermore, remember Peter's crystal clear vision of a sheet of unclean animals let down from heaven where the Lord says, "Get up, Peter. Kill and eat":

> **"Surely not, Lord!" Peter replied. "I have never eaten anything impure or unclean." The voice spoke to him a second time, "<u>Do not call anything impure that God has made clean</u>."**

This happened three times, and immediately the sheet was taken back to heaven.
Acts 10:14-16 & 11:8-10

Not only did the Lord say this to Peter three times in this vision, the incident is shared verbatim *twice* in Acts 10 and 11. Gee, do ya think the Lord's trying to get something across to us?

Frankly, citing Revelation 18:2 to support the idea that New Covenant believers must obey Old Covenant kosher laws smacks of legalistic desperation since it's not even directly addressing that topic.

'Why would believers have freedom in Christ now where they can choose what to eat and what days are more holy then others and then have that taken away in the eternal age?'

This presupposes that there will be unclean animals during the eternal age and that we will kill them for food. Neither is true. Revelation 21:4 says, "There will be no more death or mourning or crying or pain, for the old order of things has passed away."

As for holy days: We are currently living in the Church Age which exists within what the Bible calls "the present evil age" where the devil is the "god of this age" (Galatians 1:3 & 2 Corinthians 4:4). The age of the new heavens and new earth, by contrast, is our eternal "home of righteousness" (2 Peter 3:13) where the Almighty can set up any holy day — holiday — he wants, whenever he wants, and the redeemed will be blessed.

Besides, before the Israelites were given the Mosaic Law, Old Testament saints had the freedom to choose what to eat and what days were more holy than others.

'Sin means "lawlessness" so ministers who preach grace rather than Law (Torah) are supporting sin'

We addressed this argument in chapter 1, but I'd like to revisit it here because it's probably the most oft-repeated point by those who support believers being *under* the Law. This argument is so weak and obviously mistaken it's amusing. Here's why:

The New Covenant advocates **fulfilling the moral Law by walking in the spirit**. Those who walk in the spirit produce the fruit of the spirit, which are the fruits of God's very character (Galatians 5:22-23). While believers are not *under* the Law, they *fulfill* the moral Law by the spirit (Romans 8:4). As such, they're not "lawless" and therefore not guilty of sin. If Christians miss it — and we all inevitably do — we're instructed to 'fess up and God faithfully forgives, cleansing us from all unrighteousness (1 John 1:8-9). If we're cleansed from *all* unrighteousness that of course makes us righteous in God's standing, not "lawless."

As for the ceremonial Laws, they were foreshadows pointing to the Messiah. Ever since Christ manifested and fulfilled the Law they're irrelevant to the New Covenant believer in the Church Age (Colossians 2:16-17 & Galatians 3:24-25). Christians worship the Reality — Christ — not the shadows which merely pointed to the Reality. While Torah-worshippers chase shadows believers walk *with* The Reality that the shadows point to, the Mighty Christ, who **is** "The Truth" (John 14:6).

'Jesus said "If you want to enter life, keep the commandments"'

Let's read the full text of Jesus' statement, which shows the *context*:

¹⁶ Just then a man came up to Jesus and asked, "Teacher, <u>what good thing must I do to get eternal life?</u>"

¹⁷ "Why do you ask me about what is good?" Jesus replied. "There is only One who is good. <u>If you want to enter life, keep the commandments.</u>"

¹⁸ "Which ones?" he inquired.

Jesus replied, " '<u>You shall not murder, you shall not commit adultery, you shall not steal, you shall not give false testimony,</u> ¹⁹ <u>honor your father and mother,</u>' and '<u>love your neighbor as yourself.</u>' "

²⁰ "<u>All these I have kept,</u>" the young man said. "What do I still lack?"

²¹ Jesus answered, "If you want to be perfect, go, <u>sell your possessions and give to the poor</u>, and you will have treasure in heaven. <u>Then come, follow me.</u>"

²² When the young man heard this, he went away sad, because he had great wealth.

Matthew 19:16-22

The rich young man asks Christ what he has to do to obtain eternal life and Jesus responds "If you want to enter life, keep the commandments." He then lists five of the Ten Commandments, but also adds "love your neighbor as yourself," which is from Leviticus 19:18. As noted in chapter 1, the Messiah said that loving your neighbor as you love yourself is the second greatest command. This and the greatest command — loving God — comprise **the law of love** or **law of Christ**, and following this single law fulfills all the moral Law of the Old Testament (Matthew 22:34-40). In other words, Jesus was saying that if the rich young man simply followed the law of love he'd automatically fulfill the Ten Commandments, five of which he just cited.

(This statement, incidentally, proves that the Mosaic Law was more than just the Ten Commandments as the last commandment Jesus cites is not one of the Ten).

But the man wouldn't be able to fulfill the law of love in his unregenerate state. He would need a spiritual rebirth and the help of the Holy Spirit to do so. As such, Christ points the man to the Law because it would bring him to desperation and lead him to the Savior, which was the ultimate purpose of the Law.

The man's response is telling: He claimed to have kept all the Laws Christ listed and, presumably, all of the over-600 laws of the Old Covenant, which is doubtful to say the least. Operating in both common sense and the word of knowledge (1 Corinthians 12:7-11), the Lord zeroes-in on the man's arrogant self-delusion and his fleshly weakness — his great love of money. The key to walking free from these sins and apprehending eternal life was to **1. repent** of his greed, which — in practical terms — meant getting rid of the great possessions that held him in bondage (and fed his arrogance) and generously give to the poor, and **2.** follow Christ, which involves **faith**.

This is in line with the scriptural fact that **repentance/ faith** is the key to receiving eternal salvation (Acts 20:21 & Hebrews 6:1-2). Repentance isn't separate from faith; they are two sides of the same coin: Those who genuinely have faith are willing to repent and vice versa (Matthew 4:17 & John 3:16). To 'repent,' by the way, means "to change one's mind/purpose for the positive" in response to revelation from God.

'David advocated living according to God's Law (Torah)'

This argument is based on the fact that David is honored in Scripture as "a man after God's own heart" (1 Samuel 13:14 &

Acts 13:22) and, since he endorsed living according to the law (*torah*) with all one's heart, New Testament believers should as well. A few examples include Psalm 119:1, 119:34 and 19:7-11.

To begin, who said New Covenant believers *don't* live according to God's Law? The difference in our superior covenant, as explained earlier, is that Christians fulfill God's moral Law simply by walking according to their new righteous nature with the help of the Holy Spirit, our Helper (Ephesians 4:22-24, Romans 8:4 & Galatians 5:22-23). As for the kosher and ritualistic laws, again, they were shadows pointing to the Reality, Christ, and are therefore irrelevant in the Church Age.

Secondly, *torah* means more than just "Law" in the rigid sense of the Mosaic Law. *Torah* simply means "teaching" or "instruction" in the sense of pointing or indicating the way. Here's an example:

> **Listen, my son, to your father's instruction**
> **and do not forsake your mother's <u>teaching</u>** *(torah)*.
> **Proverbs 1:8**

This is an example of Hebraic parallelism where the second part of a verse restates the first part in different words. So "teaching" (*torah*) and "instruction" are synonymous terms here referring to a parent's wise counsel or tutoring.

Furthermore, notice how *torah* is used in this passage where the LORD is speaking to Isaac:

> **"I will make your descendants as numerous as the stars in the sky and will give them all these lands, and through your offspring all nations on earth will be blessed, [5] because Abraham obeyed me and did everything I required of him, keeping my commands, my decrees and my <u>instructions</u>** *(torah)*.**"**   **Genesis 26:4-5**

Abraham was our father of faith (Genesis 15:6 & Romans 4:3,11). He obeyed God's **instructions** — his *torah* — over 400 years *before* the Mosaic Law was given to Israel.

Torah can also refer to **1.** a specific or prophetic word from the LORD (Isaiah 1:10) or **2.** God's revealed word in general, which means all of the God-breathed Scriptures; that is, the Bible in general (2 Timothy 3:16). For instance, in Proverbs 29:18 *torah* is used in parallel terminology with "revelation" from God. Since New Testament believers are clearly not *under* the Old Covenant Law, but rather fulfill the moral Law by walking in the spirit, "law" (*torah*) to believers refers to God's word — revelation — that is applicable to us in our new (superior) covenant.

Thirdly, by "law" David was technically speaking of **the revealed word of God at that time**, which would've been the first five books of the Bible and other scrolls, like Job, Proverbs and the Psalms which predated David. Also, the context of David's words was *his* covenant with God, which was the *inferior* Old Covenant. Christians in the New Testament era, by contrast, are neither limited by David's inferior covenant nor the narrow amount of Scriptures of which he had access. We have a *superior* covenant (Hebrews 8:6) and the whole of the biblical canon — Genesis to Revelation — *Praise God!*

To support this, read those passages cited above where David advocated living according to the law *(torah)* and the rest of those particular psalms — Psalm 119 and Psalm 19 — and you'll observe that David used several synonyms for "law" *(torah)*, such as God's "word," "commands," "precepts," "ordinances," "decrees," "statutes" and "promises." In other words, **David was referring to God's Word in general** and, once again, to New Testament Christian this refers to the whole of Scripture, as well as any genuine word given by the Holy Spirit. So when David says "Great peace have they who love your law and nothing can make them stumble" (Psalm 119:165) this would mean the God-breathed

Scriptures in general to Christians in the context of their *superior* covenant with God, and not David's *inferior* one.

Further support can be observed in James' description of God's revealed and comprehensive Word as "the perfect **law** that gives freedom" (James 1:25 & 2:12). We know James wasn't referring *solely* to the Mosaic Law because "the letter **kills**." While the Mosaic Law is an important part of God's Word in that it defines sin and leads people to the Savior, apart from the rest of God's Word the Old Covenant is a "ministry of **death**" and a "ministry that **condemns**" (2 Corinthians 3:6-9). Indeed, the "law brings **wrath**" (Romans 4:15). The whole of God's revealed Word, by contrast, gives life and sets people free, which is why James called it "the perfect law that gives freedom."

All of this info helps us to answer this next argument…

'Torah is the way (Psalm 119:1), the truth (119:142) and the life (Deuteronomy 32:46-47); Christ is also the way, the truth and the life (John 14:6). Conclusion: Christ *is* Torah'

There are glaring problems with this simplistic argument. For one, it limits the Hebrew word *torah* to only refer to the Law of Moses; and, worse, it limits Jesus Christ — "the Word of God" (John 1:1) — to only relate to the Mosaic Law.

We saw in the previous section that *torah* doesn't only refer to the Mosaic Law and that it can more widely refer to the word/revelation of God in general, as it does in Psalm 119.

As far as the conclusion that Christ *is* Torah — the Law of Moses — this argument attempts to put the infinite Christ in a box. We know that Messiah Jesus is "the Word of God," the Creator's message to humanity. But God's message to humanity is, gratefully, far more than just the Mosaic Law. The Law's purpose was to define sin (Romans 7:7) and help humanity see its need for a Redeemer, Jesus Christ. So the Law *isn't* Christ, but rather "leads us to Christ" (Galatians 3:24). There was no redemption in the Law and, indeed, "the letter kills" (2 Corinthians 3:6). Why? Because death is the ultimate end of the Law for unregenerate people since no one can obey it in their sinful state apart from Christ. And "the wages of sin is death."

Yet God's revelation to humanity doesn't end with the Law of Moses and the corresponding death, but with the message of Christ and the corresponding reconciliation with God and eternal life (Romans 6:23 & 2 Corinthians 5:17-21). This is why the message of Christ is known as the gospel or, more literally, the "good news."

'God was angered at Israel's disregard for the Law so his solution was to send his Son to get rid of the same law?' (said with sarcasm)

'Sin' means to "miss the mark" in the sense of diverting from universal moral law (1 John 3:4). The Creator always disapproves of sin in any era in any society. It's not something unique to his dealings with Israel during the Old Testament. For instance, the very reason the land of Canaan was available for the Israelites to possess was because of God's judgment on the heathen nations thereof for their gross immorality (Leviticus 18:24-28). Hundreds of years earlier the LORD told Abraham that his descendants would possess the land of the Amorites, who dwelt in central Canaan. This possession of the land couldn't take place until then because "the sin of the Amorites had not yet reached its full measure," meaning their degree of immorality would reach the point of demanding God's judgment and thus ousting them from the land (Genesis 15:16).

What was God's purpose for giving the Law to Israel in the first place? To help humanity realize that we couldn't fulfill God's Law so that we would see our hopelessly sinful condition, which would drive us to the Savior. As it is written: "The law was brought in **so that the trespass might increase**" (Romans 5:20). So, while the LORD is always angered by immorality, God knew all along that Israel wouldn't be able to keep the Law. What Israel and humanity needed was a new nature, which is what Jesus Christ provides in the new, superior covenant (Jeremiah 31:31-33).

Speaking of this passage, here's another argument…

'Jeremiah 31:31-33 shows that the New Covenant is made with Israel not some foreign entity called "The Church" '

Let's read the passage:

³¹ "The days are coming," declares the Lord,
    "when I will make a new covenant
with the people of Israel
    and with the people of Judah.
³² It will not be like the covenant
    I made with their ancestors
when I took them by the hand
    to lead them out of Egypt,
because they broke my covenant,
    though I was a husband to them,"
declares the Lord.
³³ "This is the covenant I will make with the people of Israel
    after that time," declares the Lord.
"I will put my law in their minds
    and write it on their hearts.
I will be their God,
    and they will be my people.

                                   Jeremiah 31:31-33

This passage is indeed referring to the new covenant. The New Testament even quotes it in the book of Hebrews (8:8-12) and part of it twice (10:16-17). In Hebrews 8 it is quoted right after stressing that the new covenant is *superior* to the old one (Hebrews 8:6). Notice what is concluded:

> **By calling this covenant "new," <u>he has made the first one obsolete</u>; and what is obsolete and aging will soon disappear.**
>
> **Hebrews 8:13**

As far as the claim that the new covenant is only for Israel, anyone who argues this is blatantly violating two hermeneutical rules: "Context is king" and "Scripture interprets Scripture."

Regarding the context, Jeremiah was prophesying to the Hebrews and so used concepts relative to his audience. The LORD had given the Law to Israel, which defined sin, but they had no way to cure their sinful condition (Jeremiah 17:9).

Concerning Scripture interpreting Scripture, yes, the new covenant *started with* Christ's disciples — Hebrews — and spread throughout Jerusalem and Israel, but Peter's vision of a sheet of unclean animals let down from heaven with a voice saying, "Get up, Peter. Kill and eat" (Acts 10-11) verified to the Jewish believers that the new covenant was **for the whole world**, to which they concluded: "So then, God has granted even the Gentiles repentance unto life" (Acts 11:18). Thus Paul later said by the Holy Spirit: "There is neither Jew nor Gentile, neither slave nor free, nor is there male and female, for you are **all one in Christ Jesus**" (Galatians 3:28).

Furthermore, Gentiles who turn to the LORD through the gospel receive an *inward* circumcision via spiritual regeneration (Titus 3:5) and thus become Jews in an *inward* sense (Romans 2:29). So it's not technically erroneous for Jeremiah to say the new covenant is "with the people of Israel" (Jeremiah 31:31) because

Gentile believers are *spiritual* Jews. Meanwhile, *unrepentant* Jews, like the Pharisees and Teachers of the Law in the 1st century, are "sons of hell" *despite* their Hebraic lineage; meaning they're children of damnation regardless of their physical pedigree (Matthew 23:15 & Revelation 2:9).

As for the "Church," the Greek word for 'church' is *ekklésia (ek-klay-SEE-ah)*, which means "the called out ones." Those spiritually reborn through Christ — whether Jew or Gentile — are "called... out of darkness into his wonderful light" (1 Peter 2:9).

'Isaiah mentions the New Moon and Sabbath being observed during the eternal age of the new heavens and new earth, why would the New Moon and Sabbath be abolished just to be put back in force again?'

Let's look at the passage in question:

> **"As the new heavens and the new earth that I make will endure before me," declares the Lord, "so will your name and descendants endure. 23 From one New Moon to another and from one Sabbath to another, all mankind will come and bow down before me," says the Lord.**
> **Isaiah 66:22-23**

We have to understand the different ages, which usually correspond with the covenants God has or doesn't have with humanity. Our current age is the age of grace, the age of the New Testament or Church Age. This passage from Isaiah **concerns the eternal age of the new heavens and new earth**, detailed here in Revelation:

> **Then I saw "a new heaven and a new earth," for the first heaven and the first earth had passed away, and there was no longer any sea. [2] I saw the Holy City, the new Jerusalem, coming down out of heaven from God, prepared as a bride beautifully dressed for her husband.**
>
> **Revelation 21:1-2**

This is the eternal age that Peter instructed us to look forward to (2 Peter 3:13); it's when the heavenly city, the new Jerusalem, will come down out of heaven from God to rest on the new earth where "God's dwelling place is now among the people, and he will dwell with them" (verse 3). Notice how this is contrasted to the former ages saying, "for the first heaven and the first earth had **passed away**" (verse 1). This includes the current New Testament age, which fits into "Earth 3" in this illustration:

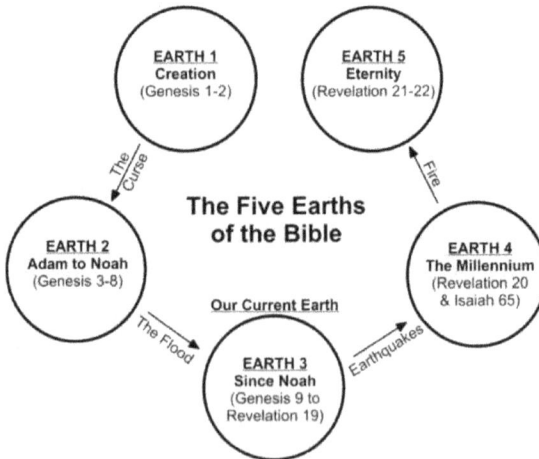

EARTH 1
Creation
(Genesis 1-2)

EARTH 5
Eternity
(Revelation 21-22)

The Curse

Fire

The Five Earths of the Bible

EARTH 2
Adam to Noah
(Genesis 3-8)

Our Current Earth

EARTH 4
The Millennium
(Revelation 20 & Isaiah 65)

The Flood

Earthquakes

EARTH 3
Since Noah
(Genesis 9 to Revelation 19)

In the eternal age of the new heavens and new earth, God's government will reign in the universe and we'll be his citizens/children/servants and, like with any government, there will be holidays — special days to celebrate or commemorate this or that — including the "New moon" and "Sabbath." Independence

Day and Thanksgiving are good examples in America. But "context is king" and **this passage is applicable to the eternal age to come** and has nothing to do with our current age of grace. Remember what the WORD OF GOD says about this current age:

> Therefore <u>do not let anyone judge you by what you eat or drink, or with regard to a religious festival, a New Moon celebration</u> or <u>a Sabbath day. These are a shadow of the things that were to come</u>; the reality, however, is found in Christ.
>
> **Colossians 2:16-17**

> But if you are <u>led by the Spirit,</u> you are <u>not under the law.</u>
>
> **Galatians 5:18**

> But now, by <u>dying to what once bound us</u>, we have been <u>released from the law</u> so that <u>we serve in the new way of the Spirit</u>, and <u>not in the old way of the written code.</u>
>
> **Romans 7:6**

> By calling <u>this covenant "new,"</u> <u>he has made the first one obsolete</u>; and what is obsolete and outdated will soon disappear.
>
> **Hebrews 8:13**

Needless to say, taking a passage from Isaiah 66 which applies to the eternal age-to-come and applying it to a wholly different earth-reality and age is an example of unsound hermeneutics. The New Testament encourages those who teach God's Word to "rightly divide" or "correctly handle" the Scriptures (2 Timothy 2:15). This of course involves applying the common sense rules of interpretation, like Context is king and Scripture interprets Scripture. When these rules are violated it always results in error.

Furthermore, the argument implies that the New Moon celebration and the Sabbath day Law were always in vogue, which simply isn't the case. We see zero evidence of these holidays until Moses gave the Israelites the Law and established the Mosaic Covenant. Before that, Adam, Eve, Cain, Noah, Abraham, Isaac, Jacob and Joseph & his brothers didn't practice these holidays, which means they weren't in function during Earth 2 and the first part of Earth 3.

As for Earth 1, which involved the work of creation and the idyllic world of Adam & Eve until their fall, it is said that God rested on the seventh day after creating the earth, universe and all physical beings, but — other than this — we have no evidence that the Sabbath was practiced during Earth 1. Why? Because — as chapter 6 showed — **Adam & Eve were in a perpetual state of paradisal Sabbath (rest) with the LORD**. They didn't have to practice the Sabbath because Earth 1 *was* the Sabbath — resting in blissful communion with the LORD — that is, once God's work of creation had ceased.

Lastly, the eternal age of the new heavens and new earth will be a wholly different reality than what we understand today. For instance, there will be no more death or pain and the redeemed will have glorified, imperishable bodies (Revelation 21:4 & 1 Corinthians 15:42-44). Wouldn't it be silly to argue that we should act now according to the way it will be in eternity? For instance, since we won't be able to die in the new heavens and new earth, should we jump off a cliff or skyscraper without a parachute? Or, since we'll be able to walk through walls like Jesus did after he received his glorified body (Luke 24:31,36-37), should we try to walk through solid objects?

The nature of reality will be completely different in eternity so it's asinine to argue that we should do now what will be done then.

'It appears that Old Testament rituals will be practiced during the Millennium, so shouldn't we practice them now?'

This refers to Ezekiel 42-46, which shows that the offerings introduced in the Levitical system will be practiced during the Millennium, such as the burnt offering, the peace offering, the sin & trespass offerings and the drink offering. Many of the feasts will also be celebrated.

The obvious response is similar to the previous argument about eternity: The nature of reality in Earth 4 — the Millennium — will be quite different than what we experience now in Earth 3 (Revelation 20:1-10). For one, the quakes that will fashion Earth 4 will be so massive that every vale will be elevated, every peak will be depressed, and every isle will be relocated (Revelation 6:12-14 & 16:17-21). Jerusalem will be raised up, and Mt. Zion will be established as chief of the mounts (Zechariah 14:10 & Micah 4:1).

More importantly, Christ will reign from Jerusalem with the assistance of glorified, immortal believers while the devil & his filthy angels will be locked up in the Abyss, unable to deceive the nations until they're released at the end. Meanwhile, mortals still alive at the end of the Tribulation and designated as "sheep" will be spiritually regenerated and allowed by Christ to enter the Millennium where they will propagate (Matthew 25:31-46). The Temple in Jerusalem will apparently be many times its current size with odd modifications.

Moreover, the laws of nature will be vastly different due to the Genesis curse being partially lifted. As such, animals will no longer eat other animals and so "the wolf will live with the lamb," "the cow will feed with the bear," "the infant will play near the hole of the cobra and the young child put his hand into the viper's nest" and "the whole earth will be full of the knowledge of the LORD" (Isaiah 11:6-9).

Furthermore, Isaiah 65:20,22 shows lifespans returning to the exceptional lengths recorded after the fall of Adam & Eve in Earth 2. These extended lifespans were possible because Earth 2 had a thick vapor sunshade which safeguarded life from the sun's ultraviolet radiation (Genesis 2:5-6 & Job 38:8-11). Our globe was like a greenhouse with dense flora growing everywhere, including the poles. The long lifespans of the Millennium in Earth 4 will likely be due to the vapor covering being restored. The planet will again have lush vegetation in great quantity (Isaiah 30:23-26 & Amos 9:13-14); even the Dead Sea will flourish (Ezekiel 47:1-9).

Getting back to the question, *why* does God allow sacrifices of the Levitical system during the Millennium since we know Christ's sacrifice made them obsolete (Hebrew 9:23-10:12)? These sacrifices will likely be a *worshipful memorial* to Christ's sacrifice, which will be in contrast to the way the Levitical system *looked forward to* the substitutionary death of the Messiah, a priest in the order of Melchizedek, not Aaron (Hebrews 7:11-12).

As with the previous argument, it's silly to contend that, just because something will be done during the Millennium, we should be doing the same now. For instance, should you allow your child to put his/her hand into a viper's next? Should ranchers allow wolves into their sheep corral? Should we trust our governments as if they were run by Jesus Christ? Obviously not.

I don't really understand this argument anyway. Is it suggesting that we should be offering the Levitical sacrifices during our current Church Age just because some will apparently be doing so during the Millennium in a memorial sense? Imagine going to your local assembly and the ministers blowing valuable time slaughtering bulls, goats and pigeons. Yeah, that'll compel the unsaved to receive the Lord (sarcasm). Think about it, not even orthodox ministers in Judaism practice the Levitical sacrifices, although they'll start doing so once the Temple is rebuilt.

When will this be? All we know from the Scriptures is that The Third Temple will be in existence when the Antichrist is revealed (2 Thessalonians 2:3-4), which will be at the halfway point of the 7-year Tribulation (Daniel 9:27). Because this will be only 3½ years into the Tribulation, theologians have determined that the Temple will probably be restored just prior to the Tribulation. After all, how else could such a glorious edifice be erected in such a short span?

This leads to our next question…

'Christ said that people alive when the Antichrist seizes power in Jerusalem should pray that their flight from Judea not take place on the Sabbath, which means the Sabbath will be observed'

This argument is based on the Messiah's end-time prophecies in Matthew 24 where he reveals that the devil-possessed Antichrist will suddenly tramp into the reconstructed Temple in Jerusalem, halt the sacrifices, curse the LORD, and pronounce himself god (Daniel 9:27 & 2 Thessalonians 2:4). Of course the Jews will be outraged by such blasphemy and so the Antichrist will turn on them with the intention of wiping them off the face of the earth. This will be his obsession during the second half of the Tribulation and this explains why Christ said this event would usher in the period of the "great tribulation," which concerns the second half of the Tribulation when excessive persecution breaks out against the Jews. Let's read the passage:

> [15] **"So when you see standing in the holy place 'the abomination that causes desolation'** [aka the Antichrist], **spoken of through the**

> prophet Daniel—let the reader understand— [16]
> then <u>let those who are in Judea flee to the
> mountains</u>. [17] Let no one on the housetop go
> down to take anything out of the house. [18] Let no
> one in the field go back to get their cloak. [19] How
> dreadful it will be in those days for pregnant
> women and nursing mothers! [20] <u>Pray that your
> flight will not take place in winter or on the
> Sabbath</u>. [21] For then there will be <u>great distress,</u>
> unequaled from the beginning of the world until
> now—and never to be equaled again.
>
> **Matthew 24:15-21**

Christ was *The* Prophet foretold in the Old Testament (Deuteronomy 18:18) and he's informing us here what it will be like in Jerusalem & Judea when the Antichrist sets himself up as god in the Temple at the midway point of the Tribulation. Of course this event would not take place for another 2000 years so the Messiah's warning is meant specifically for the corresponding Jews living in Jerusalem and surrounding Judea at that much later date.[13]

The persecution against Jews will be so great that Jesus is essentially saying "Drop everything and flee for your life!" Since leaving Jerusalem & Judea during the winter or on the Sabbath would be more difficult than other times, he's advising Jews alive in central Israel at this future time to pray that this not be so. This has nothing to do with New Covenant believers observing the Sabbath or not observing it, it's referring to the way it will be in

---

[13] Christ's words could also be viewed as a **double prophecy**, which would mean that the prophecy had *two* applications — <u>an immediate one</u> and <u>a far-flung one</u>. In this case, the more immediate application would refer to the terrible suffering that occurred in 70 A.D. when Jerusalem was destroyed by Roman troops. Being only 37 years in the future, the (double) prophecy would therefore be relevant to Jesus' listeners.

Jerusalem & Judea during the mid-Tribulation when the Antichrist sets himself up as god and issues legal orders to apprehend and kill all Jews. If you find this incredulous, this very thing happened on a lesser scale in Nazi-controlled Europe during World War II, which wasn't all that long ago.

As far as his reference to the Sabbath goes, even today it's more difficult to travel in secularized Jerusalem on the Sabbath because of the lack of transportation — whether buses, trains, planes or taxi service — how much more so during the Tribulation when the Temple is rebuilt and there's increased religious fervor with the Levitical sacrifices reinstituted? (We know they will be reinstituted because Daniel 9:27 says the Antichrist will immediately put a stop to the sacrifices & offerings when he seizes power in Jerusalem).

Honestly, this argument is tantamount to grasping for straws.

Let's close this chapter with this curious contention…

'James said "faith without deeds is dead" (James 2:17,26) '

I'm confused as to how this in any way supports Christians being under the Mosaic Law. James was simply pointing out that genuine faith produces results because it's more than just mental assent. He certainly wasn't saying that works produce salvation because it is clearly established elsewhere in Scripture that we're saved by God's graciousness through faith "not by works so that no one can boast" (Ephesians 2:8-9). This famous passage is followed-up by something that wholly agrees with what James wrote: "For we are God's workmanship, created in Christ Jesus to do good works" (Ephesians 2:10). Again, genuine faith produces the corresponding works, but this is different than saying that works produce salvation, which is human religion. Let's not get the cart before the horse!

Getting back to James 2, the context reveals all: Before emphasizing that faith without deeds is dead he says "If you really keep **the royal law** found in scripture, '**Love your neighbor as yourself**,' you are doing right" (verse 8). We observed in chapter 1 and elsewhere that this "royal law" is the **law of Christ**, the **law of love** through which New Covenant believers fulfill the moral Law by the Spirit. We saw how Jesus gave this command in his response to an Expert in the Law (Matthew 22:37-40), as well as to his disciples at the Last Supper (John 13:34-35 & 14:11,15). It's repeatedly emphasized in the New Testament that fulfilling this law of love automatically fulfills all the moral commands of the Law and the Prophets (Matthew 7:12, Romans 13:8-10 & Galatians 5:14).

Not to be misunderstood, James offers practical examples of following the law of love: Looking after orphans and widows in their distress, as well as providing for the needy (James 1:27 & 2:14-17). If we have the love of God in us we'll naturally help such people as long as it's in our power to do so; if not, we'll ignore them.

This is wonderful stuff, but it's in no way saying we're saved by works or that we're under the Mosaic Law.

Wrap Up

These are the best arguments advocates for being *under* the Law can come up with and — as you can see — they hold no water and are easily countered. Further objections are just variations on the same sincere-but-sincerely-wrong themes.

12

Closing Word

Our Scripture-based conclusion is that believers in Christ are not *under* the Old Testament Law, but rather *fulfill* the moral law by living out of our new nature, which was "created to by like God in true righteousness and holiness" with the help & guidance of the Holy Spirit.

The Sabbath day law, the Jewish holidays and dietary laws have ceased because they were mere shadows pointing to the Reality — the Truth — Jesus Christ. And we are *in* Christ. We have a *superior* covenant with God, why go backwards to an *inferior* one? Only an uninformed fool would do so.

Let me close by reiterating something important Paul pointed out: "He has made us competent as ministers of a <u>new covenant</u> — not of the letter but of the Spirit; for **the letter kills**, but **the Spirit gives life**" (2 Corinthians 3:6). He goes on to describe the <u>old covenant</u> in terms of "the ministry that brought **death**" and "the ministry that brought **condemnation**." Why is the covenant of the Law described in these terms? Because without spiritual rebirth through Christ, condemnation & death are the end result of the inferior old covenant.

Paul then drives home one of the most important qualities of our superior new covenant:

> **Now the Lord is the Spirit, and where the Spirit of the Lord is, <u>there is freedom</u>.**
> **2 Corinthians 3:17**

Praise the LORD! We are FREE from the Law:

> **<u>It is for freedom that Christ has set us free</u>. Stand firm, then, and do not let yourselves be burdened again by a yoke of slavery.**
> **Galatians 5:1**

The "yoke of slavery" refers to the yoke of the Mosaic Law. New Covenant believers are FREE from this yoke; and the yoke of religious laws/traditions in general. We're also FREE from the yoke of the flesh, the sinful nature. *Praise God!*

Amen and Amen.

For important details on legalism and its various forms, please see my companion-book *Legalism Unmasked*.

Bibliography

Brown, Francis/Driver, S.R./Briggs, Charles A. *Brown-Driver-Briggs Lexicon.* Peabody: Hendrickson Publishers, 1994

Bullinger, Ethelbert W. *A Critical Lexicon and Concordance to the English and Greek New Testament.* Grand Rapids: Zondervan Publishing House, 1975

Epp, Theodore H. *What does God's Word say about the Christian keeping the Sabbath?* Retrieved from https://www.backto thebible.org/what-does-god-s-word-say-about-the-christian-keeping-the-sabbath, (no date)

Helps Word-Studies Lexicon. Retrieved from Biblehub.com. 1987, 2011

Houdmann, S. Michael. *Got Questions?* Retrieved from https://www.gotquestions.org/, 2002-2018

LORD, The. *Berean Study Bible (BSB).* Bible Hub, 2016

LORD, The. *English Standard Version (ESV). Holy Bible.* Chicago: Crossway, 2001

LORD, The. *Good News Translation. Holy Bible.* The Bible Society, 2001

LORD, The. *International Standard Version. Holy Bible.* Davidson Press, 1999

LORD, The. *King James Version. Holy Bible.* Iowa Falls: World Bible Publishers

LORD, The. *New American Standard Bible. Holy Bible.* Nashville: Holman, 1977

LORD, The. *New International Version. Holy Bible.* Nashville: Holman, 1986

LORD, The. *New International Version (Revised). Holy Bible.* Nashville: Holman, 2011

LORD, The. *New King James Version Study Bible: Second Edition.* Nashville: Thomas Nelson, 2012

LORD, The. *New Living Translation.* Carol Stream: Tyndale House Publishers, 2006

LORD, The. New Revised Standard Version. Holy Bible. Nashville: Nelson, 1989

LORD, The. *The Amplified Bible.* Grand Rapids: Zondervan, 1987

LORD, The. *Quest Study Bible: New International Version.* Grand Rapids: Zondervan, 2003

LORD, The. *World English Bible (WEB).* Salt Lake City: Project Gutenberg, 2013

LORD, The. *Weymouth New Testament.* Ulan Press, 2012

LORD, The. *Young's Literal Translation (YLT).* Grand Rapids: Baker Books, 1989

Reagan, David. *The Earth in Prophecy: Eternal Restoration or Fiery Finish?* Retrieved from http://christinprophecy.org/articles/the-earth-in-prophecy/, 2018

Reagan, David. *The Rise and Fall of the Antichrist.* Retrieved from http://christinprophecy.org/articles/the-rise-and-fall-of-the-anti christ/, 2018

Strong, James. *Strong's Exhaustive Concordance.* Grand Rapids: Baker, 1991

Vine, W.E. *Vine's Expository Dictionary of Biblical Words.* Cambridge: Nelson, 1985

White, Chris. *Should Christians Observe the Sabbath.* CWM, 2013

Yandian, Bob. *Galatians—The Spirit-Controlled Life.* Tulsa: Harrison House, 1985

Fountain of Life

Teaching Ministry

(Psalm 36:9)

The mission of Fountain of Life is to **set the captives FREE** by **reaching the world** with the **life-changing truths of God's Word**, the **power of the Holy Spirit** and the **Awesome News of the message of Jesus Christ**.

We're calling Spiritual Warriors all over the Earth to partner with us on this mission!

Books by Dirk Waren:

The Believer's Guide to Forgiveness & Warfare
Legalism Unmasked
HELL KNOW!
SHEOL KNOW!
The Four Stages of Spiritual Growth
ANGELS: Their Purpose and Your Responsibility
THE LAW and the Believer

www.ingramcontent.com/pod-product-compliance
Lightning Source LLC
Chambersburg PA
CBHW060508030426
42337CB00015B/1791